Spinoza's Theory of Truth

Spinoza's Theory of Truth

THOMAS CARSON MARK

Columbia University Press
New York and London · 1972

Library of Congress Cataloging in Publication Data

Mark, Thomas Carson, 1941–
    Spinoza's theory of truth.

    Bibliography: p. 129–32
    1. Spinoza, Benedictus de, 1632–1677.
2. Truth.   I. Title.
B3999.T7M3   111.8′3   72-3721
ISBN 0-231-03621-3

Foreword

I AM ADDING a short foreword to Thomas Mark's *Spinoza's Theory of Truth*, but not because I think that I can add anything to the substance or merit of the book, which I trust will stand its own ground before its readers and critics. Mr. Mark has had the courage to choose for his subject a great and difficult thinker on whom a good deal has been written, and he has shown the ability to make a valuable and novel contribution to our understanding of this thinker.

Among the many concepts and problems of Spinoza's philosophy, his theory of truth has received comparatively little attention, and the treatment of this problem has led to an impasse because of the uncritical assumption that truth must be understood either as a kind of coherence or of correspondence. In drawing on the relevant passages in the *Ethics*, Mr. Mark has convinced me that Spinoza's theory of truth is not reducible to either one of those conventional alternatives but has a meaning of its own that includes several aspects of the ancient, "ontological" conception of truth.

In pursuing this task, Mr. Mark has not only supplied a more convincing interpretation of one special detail in Spinoza's philosophy. . . . he has also shown that the concept of truth has a central importance in Spinoza's thought and is closely related to such other basic notions as substance and freedom. Mark has thus given us a new insight into Spinoza's thought as a whole, viewing it from a perspective that had been neglected.

By showing that the ancient relationship between truth and being is still alive in a thinker like Spinoza, Mark has also opened up the way for a new and more ambitious historical and philosophical undertaking: a history of the concept of truth, and especially of ontological truth, in Western thought from the Greeks to the present. I hope that Mr. Mark himself will pursue this broader investigation, after he has formulated the problem and successfully resolved it in one important instance.

Paul Oskar Kristeller

New York, Columbia University
May 6, 1972

Preface

IN QUOTING FROM the works of Spinoza, I have normally given the original Latin text, as well as an English translation. Occasionally, however, where the passage quoted seemed more illustrative than central to my argument, and where there could be no question as to the accuracy of the translation, I have taken the liberty of giving the text in English only.

Quotations in Latin are taken from *Spinoza Opera*, ed. Carl Gebhardt (Heidelberg, 1925). Page references following Latin quotations give the volume and page numbers in this edition. Quotations in English are taken, with occasional modifications, from:

Ethics Preceded by On the Improvement of the Understanding, ed. James Gutman, New York, 1949. The translation of the *Ethics* is by G. W. H. White, revised by Amelia H. Stirling. That of *On the Improvement of the Understanding* is by R. H. M. Elwes.

The Correspondence of Spinoza, ed. A. Wolf, London, 1966.
Spinoza's Short Treatise on God, Man, & His Well Being, ed.
A. Wolf, New York, 1963.

Page references following English quotations give page numbers in these editions. All passages from the *Ethics* are identified not by page but by part and proposition number, abbreviated and placed in parentheses following the passage quoted, thus: (E-I, 1). The *Tractatus de Intellectus Emendatione (On the Improvement of the Understanding)* is abbreviated throughout as *TdIE.*

I have omitted publication data from the footnotes; it can be found in the bibliography.

The portrait of Spinoza that appears as frontispiece is published here for the first time. Modeled on the well-known engraving that appears in some copies of Spinoza's *Opera Posthuma,* it is a drawing, in brown ink, signed "J. Faber 1691." In the eighteenth century, the drawing was inserted into a copy of Spinoza's *Nagelate Schriften* that was found in Amsterdam in 1972. That copy is now in the private collection of Salomon S. Meyer, in Amsterdam, and the portrait is reproduced with his permission.

John Faber was born in the Hague, sometime between 1650 and 1660. He was active for a time in the Netherlands, and then, after 1695, in London. He died in Bristol in 1721. His drawings are reasonably numerous; they usually represent prominent people of the time, and are modeled on engravings (occasionally on paintings) by other artists. A second Faber drawing of Spinoza is known. Dated 1692 and derived, like this one, from the *Opera Posthuma* engraving, it hangs in the Bibliotheca Rosenthaliana in Amsterdam.

Acknowledgments

I AM GRATEFUL to Jeannette Haien Ballard, who provided ideal conditions for preliminary work on this study, and to Dorothea Wender, for special assistance in preparing the manuscript; also to Justus Buchler and Arthur C. Danto, who read the manuscript and gave me the benefit of their comments. Most of all, I am grateful for the sustained encouragement and support of Paul Oskar Kristeller.

•

Contents

Spinoza's Theory of Truth

I. Introduction

WHEN PEOPLE TALK about truth, the discussion often deals with the definition of truth; in particular, it is asked whether truth means correspondence or coherence. Thus, if we ask about a person's theory of truth, we may be taken to be asking whether the person maintains a correspondence theory or a coherence theory. This question, asked about Spinoza, has been variously answered. The most common position, represented by such writers as Joachim, Hampshire, and Roth, is that he had a coherence theory, although some, like Parkinson and Curley, have denied this or at least questioned it. Evidence for both theories can be found in the *Ethics,* and even if we conclude that one of them is pre-eminent, we ought, nevertheless, to be able to account for the presence of the other. It is possible that neither a coherence theory nor a correspondence theory, in any of their common interpretations, can adequately describe Spinoza's position.

In the secondary literature on Spinoza there is, so far as I have discovered, rather little by way of argumentative discussion of Spinoza's definition of truth. We are told that he held a coherence theory, but we are not usually offered a thorough examination of the reasons for attributing the coherence theory to him, or an explanation of what the coherence theory means. Consequently, when commentators say that Spinoza held a coherence theory, it is not clear just what position is being described, or what the reasons are for thinking that Spinoza held it. The coherence theory of truth is treated as something with which we can be presumed to have independent and prior acquaintance.

If we *are* expected to be antecedently acquainted with the coherence theory, it is reasonable to ask, without here having Spinoza particularly in mind, just what is generally meant when people talk of the coherence theory of truth. We find that the theory is most commonly associated with idealist philosophers of the nineteenth and twentieth centuries, men like Bradley, Joachim, and Blanshard. Its supporters do not agree on every detail, but in subsequent discussion I propose that the coherence theory be taken to include the following four theses, which would be accepted in some form, I believe, by most if not all of its defenders.

1) Truth (usually applied to ideas or judgments) is defined as coherence within the orderly system that constitutes reality.

2) The criterion, as well as the definition, of truth is coherence within the ordered system of reality.

3) Relations are internal; that is, a thing's relations with other things are essential to its being what it is; indeed, they may *constitute* what it is.

4) Truth admits of degrees. Instead of being true or false, individual ideas or judgments are partly true or partly false.

No idea except perhaps the idea of the whole (and therefore no idea that a human being could grasp) can properly be said to be wholly true.[1]

If the position I have sketched here is what most people understand by the coherence theory, then we can only suppose that this is what commentators have in mind when they tell us without further qualification that Spinoza held a coherence view. It may appear peculiar that this idealist theory should be attributed to Spinoza, and I do, myself, think that it is anachronistic. It seems to me that among some writers on Spinoza—Lévêque and Joachim are the ones I shall discuss in particular—there has been a tendency to present Spinoza as too much of an idealist, and one aspect of this "idealization" of Spinoza is the attribution to him of the coherence theory of truth. The effect of this has been to distract attention from Spinoza's relation to the much older theory of truth as being, or ontological truth. In my opinion, the view of truth as being offers a much more promising approach to Spinoza's views on truth than does the coherence theory. I shall discuss these issues in Chapter IV.

We have supposed, so far, that the theory of truth can be discussed and criticized by itself, without much explicit discussion of the rest of Spinoza's philosophy, a kind of supposition made nowadays without much question. Much analytic philosophy is carried on in the belief that the most effective way of dealing with problems is to isolate them as far as possible, and then to solve each one individually. But this procedure rests on a metaphysical assumption that Spinoza would deny. He did not think that one could speak intelligibly about any subject matter without some grasp of its relation to the rest of reality. Accordingly, he gives us a rather fully-developed metaphysics, epistemology, and psychology in what

---

[1] The best discussion and defense of the theory that I know is by Brand Blanshard in *The Nature of Thought*, chapters 25–27.

is supposed to be a work on ethics. One consequence of this point of view is that if we are to understand Spinoza's theory of truth as he might wish it understood, we must place it in the context of his metaphysical system. It seems to me desirable, therefore, to offer some discussion of the metaphysical doctrines that provide a context in which truth can be understood, and of certain terminology that will be important later on. This is the purpose of the next chapter. I do not pretend to give a comprehensive account of Spinoza's metaphysics; there are important issues that I shall not even mention. Nevertheless, I shall try to describe the issues that I do treat in a way that does not presuppose extensive knowledge of Spinoza. In addition to giving necessary preparation for understanding Spinoza's conception of truth, the discussion of his general orientation will, I hope, provide a context in terms of which we can afterwards describe the position of the concept of truth in Spinoza's system. That position is, I believe, logically much more central than it has usually been made out to be.

We have observed that although Spinoza is writing primarily about ethics, he brings in other topics too because he believes them to be pertinent to a discussion of ethics. Since Spinoza usually includes only as much as he considers indispensable, leaving the rest "for another treatise," it is at least plausible that the theory of truth is discussed in the *Ethics* because of its relevance to ethical matters. And indeed, when we turn to parts IV and V of the *Ethics* it turns out that truth and knowledge are of central importance in the life that Spinoza regards as desirable. An important part, therefore, of Spinoza's theory of truth as described in the *Ethics* is its application in attaining the good life. Unless we understand its operation here, as well as its purely epistemological features, we will not understand all that Spinoza claimed for his theory.

It seems, therefore, that there are three important kinds of questions to discuss concerning Spinoza's theory of truth. First of all, we must explain the theory itself, taking up such issues as the definition and criterion of truth. Then we may ask how the theory fits into Spinoza's metaphysics. The metaphysical importance of the theory of truth will emerge fairly easily from the discussion of truth itself, and these two issues occupy most of chapters III and IV. Finally, we can ask how the theory of truth relates to ethics, the assumption being that if it had no ethical significance at all it would not receive the attention it does in the *Ethics*. The ethical significance of the theory of truth is taken up in Chapter V.

My account is based on Spinoza's views as we have them in the *Ethics*, and, to a lesser extent, as we have them in the *Tractatus de Intellectus Emendatione*. I do refer, of course, to other works of Spinoza, but I have made no systematic attempt to compare the theory of truth as expressed in the *Ethics* with what Spinoza says about truth in his other works. This is not an essay about the development of Spinoza's thought. Rather, it is about the concept of truth and its importance in the final version of Spinoza's philosophy. It is in the *Ethics* that we have an authoritative statement of his philosophy, and so the *Ethics* will form the basis of our discussion.

II. Preliminary topics

a. Substance, mode, and attribute

THE CONCEPT OF SUBSTANCE has a long history, which can be traced through the Middle Ages and which goes back ultimately to Aristotle. For Aristotle, substance is what exists "independently," or is "separable," or is "in itself." [1] A physical object can be used to illustrate what this means (without suggesting that for Aristotle "substance" and "physical object" are synonymous). A physical object is self-contained, in that it can be supposed, on the level of common sense, to have its own identity and to exist unaffected by changes that may go on around it. To use Aristo-

---

[1] "Some things can exist apart and some cannot, and it is the former that are substances" (Aristotle, *Metaphysics* XII, 5, 1070b36). Wolfson quotes numerous medieval formulations of the distinction between substance and accident (*The Philosophy of Spinoza*, I, 62–64).

telian language, it is primarily to physical objects that we attribute existence or being in the full sense. A color, on the other hand, cannot exist alone; there must be a physical object that *has* the color. Thus, a color is not a substance. A physical object exists "in itself"; color, location, and other "accidental" properties occur in objects, not in themselves.

But Spinoza did not derive his conception of substance from Aristotle. The term was widely used in the seventeenth century by writers of varying persuasions, and although it was sometimes interpreted along Aristotelian lines there were other interpretations as well. Nevertheless, the idea of being "in itself" was one of the standard conceptions; thus, we find Descartes speaking of "une substance, ou bien une chose qui de soi est capable d'exister." [2]

Spinoza agrees that substance is to be defined as whatever exists in itself:

§ By substance I understand that which is in itself and is conceived through itself; in other words, that the conception of which does not need the conception of another thing from which it must be formed. (E-I, def. 3)

Per substantiam intelligo id, quod in se est, & per se concipitur: hoc est id, cujus conceptus non indiget conceptu alterius rei, a quo formari debeat.

[2] *Meditation III*, in *Oeuvres Philosophiques*, ed. Ferdinand Alquié, vol. II, p. 444. The translation is that of the French edition of 1647, and it was approved by Descartes himself. Since Descartes made certain additions and modifications in the text (without, however, changing the original sense, according to Alquié, p. 379), some commentators (Bouillet, for example), consider this French text to be preferable to the Latin. The Latin text reads as follows: ". . . esse substantiam, sive esse rem quae per se apta est existere" (p. 199). Alquié supplies references to the edition of Adam and Tannery: IX, 35 (French); VII, 44 (Latin).

This is not the *only* way Descartes speaks of substance. E. M. Curley offers an interesting discussion of various seventeenth-century accounts of substance, giving particular attention to Descartes (*Spinoza's Metaphysics*, pp. 5–20).

But he does not think that physical objects satisfy the definition. For every physical object has a cause, and if an object is caused by another object, can we say, strictly, that the caused object exists *independently?* An *in*dependent thing could not *depend* on any cause and still be independent. So, if something is influenced or changed by something else, then it is not "in itself," or "separable," and if the cause has a cause of its own, then *it* is not strictly independent either. Since every physical object has a cause, no physical object is a substance.

Spinoza claims that when we apply the definition of substance strictly, we discover that nothing satisfies the definition except the universe taken as a whole. It always makes sense to look for the cause of a physical object, but if we tried to give a *complete* causal explanation we could not stop short of a description of the entire system of physical existence. Only the whole universe can exist "in itself." It does not make sense to look for the cause of the universe, taking the universe as the totality of what is. For the cause of the universe would have to *be*, and so the cause itself would be included under "the totality of what is." There can *be* nothing outside the totality of what is, so there is nothing on which the totality could depend—nothing that could be called its cause: "This [the first principle of Nature] is, in fact, a being single and infinite; in other words, it is the sum total of being, beyond which there is no being found" (*TdIE*, p. 26). Thus, there can be only one substance. Substance is the universe as a whole, or the totality of what is. Anything that is not the whole must be part of the whole—it exists *in* the whole.

Spinoza goes on to link the totality of nature—substance—with "God." Obviously, if the word "God" refers to the substance we have been describing, the conception of God must be different from the one encountered in Christian and Jewish theology. On the other hand, it turns out that *some* of the characteristics traditionally assigned to God—eternity, for example—can be given interpretations in Spinoza's system. It is always important, therefore, to remember that when Spinoza talks, say, of God's power, he means something very special, something that, despite verbal similarity, is not necessarily found in earlier religious philosophy.[3]

We have described Spinoza as if he were undertaking an essentially Aristotelian investigation of being, first establishing a definition of substance and then proceeding to look for things that could satisfy the definition. The historical accuracy of an account that makes an Aristotelian of Spinoza is

[3] It has been suggested that to use "God" in such a peculiar manner is to give up religion altogether; one cannot use "God" and "nature" as synonyms, it is claimed, and still have a religious philosophy. It has been further suggested that Spinoza uses the word "God" only to appease some of his contemporaries (Wolfson, *The Philosophy of Spinoza*, I, 177), and that the word "God" was substituted in places where the word "nature" appeared in earlier drafts of the *Ethics* (A. M. Deborin, "Spinoza's World View," p. 102). The substitution theory is made implausible, it seems to me, by the occurrence in the *Ethics* of both "God" and "nature," and the famous phrase "deus sive natura" is especially damaging to the theory. Surely if Spinoza had wanted to pull the wool over people's eyes he could have done a more thorough job. But the other suggestion, that Spinoza abandons religion completely, using "God" primarily as an appeasing term, calls for two remarks: (1) Despite its novelty, Spinoza's God *can* be an object of religious feeling, since it *was* so for Spinoza. Whether or not we share his beliefs, and whether or not we understand every detail of his philosophy, no one, I think, who reads Part V of the *Ethics* can doubt either Spinoza's sincerity or the religious nature of his feelings. Furthermore, (2) the terms "God" and "nature" are *not* synonymous for Spinoza. They do refer to the same thing—they have the same extension—but from that it does not follow that they have the same meaning. The words have different associations for Spinoza, just as they have in ordinary Latin. He speaks of "amor intellectualis Dei," not "amor intellectualis naturae," not because "Deus" and "natura" do not refer to the same thing (they do), but because "natura" does not have the religious significance of "Deus."

The unity of substance, and the identification of God and nature are not altogether without precedent; they occur, for example, in Bruno. Many commentators have believed that Bruno was an important influence on Spinoza; this seems, however, to be something that cannot be established with certainty. See Stanislaus von Dunin-Borkowski, *Spinoza*, vol. I: *Der junge DeSpinoza*, 2nd ed. pp. 239 f.; also pp. 481 f.

open to question, particularly in view of Spinoza's disparaging remarks about Aristotle,[4] although some writers, notably Wolfson, have regarded Aristotle as an important influence on Spinoza (the influence is transmitted, often, through medieval Aristotelians). In any case, the approach we have taken does bring out one of the fundamental distinctions in Spinoza's metaphysics, the distinction between what is in itself and what is not in itself. We have seen that Spinoza's term for what is in itself is "substance"; what is not in itself he calls "mode" or "modification":

§ By mode I understand the modifications of substance, or that which is in another thing through which it must be conceived. (E-I, def. 5)

Per modum intelligo substantiae affectiones, sive id, quod in alio est, per quod etiam concipitur.

Individual physical objects are "modes" for Spinoza. We have seen above that the causal description of a physical object cannot be anything less than the complete description of physical reality, thus every physical object is "in another thing through which it must be conceived." Everything is either a substance or a mode:

§ Everything that is, is either in itself or in another. (E-I, Axiom 1)

Omnia, quae sunt, vel in se, vel in alio sunt.

The relation between substance and mode may appear to be simply another version of the Aristotelian distinction between a substance and its accidents, but that is not an altogether satisfactory explanation.[5] Modes are accidents of sub-

---

[4] "The authority of Plato, Aristotle, and Socrates has not much weight with me" (Letter LVI, p. 290).

[5] In some early writings Spinoza does use the word "accident;" see, for instance, Letter IV. Later "accident" is dropped in favor of "mode" or "modification."

stance in the sense that they are not part of its *definition;*
they do not constitute the essence of substance (their definition, in fact, is exactly the opposite of the definition of substance), and so they are "accidents of substance." But in another sense they are not accidents at all. Substance, as we
have seen, can be identified with the totality of what is.
Clearly if the totality were altered in any respect, it would no
longer be exactly the same totality that it is. That is to say,
God's nature would be altered: God would not be God. Such
a thing is obviously impossible, according to Spinoza, and so
in this sense there is nothing "accidental" or contingent about
the modifications of substance. They *must* be what they are if
substance is to be what it is.

A second important distinction in Spinoza is the one between substance and attribute. We can bring this out as follows. Instead of portraying Spinoza asking "what is substance?" and proceeding from a definition to a search for
examples, we can present him asking a different sort of question: "What are the most comprehensive characteristics of
being?" That is, "What are the most inclusive terms, or categories, that can be used to describe what is?" This sort of inquiry might go like this: starting with individual things, like
tables and chairs, we can move to the more general category
"furniture," and ultimately to "physical object." We can talk
about the properties that physical objects have in common, or
rather, we can talk of the properties of physical existence as
such. Physical existence is characterized by existence in
space: it presents itself as spatial existence. One "comprehensive characteristic of being," therefore, is physical existence in
space.

But not all being is in space, which means that not all
being is physical. We talk of ideas or concepts, and they do
not enter into spatial relations. It is as good a use of the word
"is" to say that a thought *is* as to say that a body *is;* "being"

can be understood in either way, and each way is as much a revelation of what *being* is as the other. Thus, we find ourselves presented with two fundamental sorts of things, which we call "thoughts" and "bodies," or "the mental" and "the physical," or "mind" and "matter," and the two sorts of things do not appear to be reducible one to the other. Under the heading "everything that is," we must include both thoughts and bodies. Spinoza's way of expressing this is to say that substance has two "attributes," the attribute of Thought and the attribute of Extension. Bodies, or physical existence, represent being "conceived under the attribute of Extension," and ideas or mental existence represent being "conceived under the attribute of Thought." *Being* is expressed in each case, but it is expressed in a different way. This terminology —"thought" and "extension"—is Cartesian (earlier writers would have used terms like "matter" and "form," or "body" and "soul"), but whereas Descartes speaks of "thinking substance" and "extended substance," Spinoza does not consider Thought and Extension to be substances.

Neither Thought nor Extension is prior to the other. Ideas are not copies of bodies, with a kind of secondary and dependent existence, nor are bodies reflections of ideas in any sense that would make them subsidiary to ideas. Spinoza is neither a materialist nor an idealist.[6] Thought and Extension are simply the two ways in which we can talk about what is. We think of things as being either thoughts or bodies; their status as thought or as physical body seems to us to be the most fundamental feature of their being at all. We can make no

---

[6] He has been interpreted in both ways, however. Joachim and Lévêque, among others, treat him as an idealist (discussed below, chapters III and IV), whereas he was attacked in the seventeenth century, and he is praised today in the Soviet Union, for being a materialist and an atheist. Examples of Soviet views of Spinoza may be found in George L. Kline, ed., *Spinoza in Soviet Philosophy*.

more general classification of a thing, except simply to say "it *is*." In Spinoza's terms:

§ By attribute I understand that which the intellect perceives of substance as constituting its essence. (E-I, def. 4)

Per attributum intelligo id, quod intellectus de substantia percipit, tanquam ejusdem essentiam constituens.[7]

Joachim puts this as follows: "What is ultimately real manifests for our intelligence an 'extended' and a 'thinking' character."[8] This is described by Wolfson as "the invention by

---

[7] Although "constituting" is the most common rendering, Jonathan Bennett has suggested that *constituens* ought to be translated as "characterize," "apply to," or "instantiating." He says that "The word *constituere*, as the translators might have learned from a good dictionary, can bear that meaning, and in this context it must do so" ("A Note on Descartes and Spinoza," p. 380). Bennett does not cite "a good dictionary," but the standard ones (Cassell's; Lewis & Short) do not, in fact, offer the meaning he suggests. But even if they did, that would not establish Bennett's point. For whatever one's views on the purpose of a dictionary of a spoken language such as English, a dictionary of a purely literary language like Latin can serve only to describe the usage of people who wrote in that language. Thus, if we *did* find the meaning that Bennett suggests, all we could conclude would be that *some* Latin writer used *constituere* in that way. At the very least, Bennett would have to show that the usage occurred in writers Spinoza might have known.

The issue here, I think, is a confusion between interpretation and translation. The interpretation of Spinoza's attributes is a debated question, and as an interpretation Bennett's suggestion may be defensible, although he does not explain it in enough detail to permit evaluation. It may (depending on what he really means) receive some confirmation from *TdIE*, where Spinoza speaks of "attributes of God displaying his essence" (*TdIE*, p. 26n), "attributa Dei, quae ostendunt ipsius essentiam" (II, 29, note z). But Bennett proposes to settle matters of interpretation by pretending that they are matters of translation, whereas the aim of a good translator surely is to give a rendering that is neutral as regards different interpretations that can be legitimately placed on the text. Bennett's view is attacked, for interpretative reasons, and the standard translation defended, by Alan Donagan, "A Note on Spinoza, Ethics, I, 10."

[8] *A Study of the Ethics of Spinoza*, p. 21.

the mind of certain universal terms, referred to as attributes, to describe the actions or power of substance." [9]

But although we can discriminate only thoughts and bodies, it does not follow that there are no other ways in which being could be expressed. Humans happen to think in terms of mental and physical existence—in Spinoza's terms, we know two attributes of God or substance—but God has infinitely many attributes. Substance *could* be apprehended in other ways, by intellects different from ours.

The doctrine of infinite attributes raises problems of interpretation which, fortunately, need not concern us here. It is important to remember, though, that despite our ignorance of some attributes, those that we know do, by definition, constitute the *essence* of God. Now substance is defined as that which is in itself. Thus, if we conceive the essence of substance, it is precisely this "in itselfness" that we should conceive. "In itselfness" can be variously glossed as "completeness of being," or "complete being," and it is, I think, part of what is conveyed by the term "causa sui." If an attribute expresses the essence of God, that means that we can conceive a complete and independent being under that attribute; we can conceive, say, physical existence that is perfectly self-contained, complete, and independent. (In the case of physical existence, we have seen that this concept is instantiated only by the universe as a whole.) But there is nothing in the *definition* of substance—being in itself—that limits its instantiation to physical or mental being. It just happens that humans think of being in only two ways. [10]

9 "Spinoza's Mechanism, Attributes, and Panpsychism," p. 310. This interpretation of the attributes has been attacked; see, for instance, Grace A. de Laguna's review of Wolfson's *The Philosophy of Spinoza*, pp. 290–91.

10 My interpretation of the essence of God, which emphasizes "causa sui" and "being in itself," should not be taken as a complete account of Spinoza's concept of the essence of God. Some of Spinoza's statements

The distinction between substance and attribute is not the same as the distinction between substance and mode (or modification). Modes are ordinarily finite expressions of substance; they exist in substance, asserting or representing a particular, limited portion of the infinite complexity of what completely is. They are not, strictly speaking, modifications of *attributes,* although Spinoza does permit himself to speak of modes of Thought and modes of Extension. It would be more accurate to speak, as he also does, of modes of substance conceived under (or through) different attributes. Individual thoughts, or "ideas," are modes of substance conceived through Thought; bodies are modes of substance conceived through Extension.

Physical objects enter into relations with other physical objects, and ideas with other ideas. Thus, bodies are caused by other bodies, and thoughts are caused by other thoughts. It would be nonsense to talk of a cause and effect relation between thoughts and bodies. "The body cannot determine the mind to thought, neither can the mind determine the body to motion and rest, nor to anything else if there be anything else" (E-III, 2). God, or being, is a single system, which can be expressed or conceived in any number of ways, but it is unintelligible to leap from one form of expression to another. ". . . when things are considered as modes of thought we must explain the order of the whole of Nature or the connec-

---

about God's essence seem unrelated to the view I have offered; for instance: "His intellect and His will are not distinguishable from His essence . . ." (E-I, 33, note #2), or "The power of God is his essence itself" (E-I, 34). I do not think that these statements need be taken as refutations of the view I have offered of God's essence, but a full explanation would be very lengthy. All I wish to claim here is that (1) my interpretation fits many of Spinoza's statements and, in particular, the ones where he is most likely to be careful in his terminology (e.g. the definitions), and (2) adopting "causa sui" as the central concept in Spinoza's view of substance lets us draw a number of conclusions about the concepts of truth and freedom. These conclusions appear in chapters III and IV, below.

tion of causes by the attribute of thought alone, and when things are considered as modes of extension, the order of the whole of Nature must be explained through the attribute of extension alone, and so with other attributes" (E-II, 7, note). Each form of expression is complete; everything that is can be expressed under any attribute. The attributes are equivalent ways of expressing what is, and there are indefinitely many of them. Spinoza puts this by saying that effects follow "in infinite ways" from substance. Since, in addition to the infinitely many attributes, there are also infinitely many modifications of substance, Spinoza says that "infinite numbers of things in infinite ways must follow" (E-I, 16).

When we give explanations of, say, physical objects, we are tracing relations between physical objects. Although physical objects are only one way of expressing reality, their relations are genuine, and they do give us information about reality. Still, we could just as well trace the relations between ideas. There too, we have genuine relations, which tell us something about reality. The ideas, in their relations to one another, are one aspect of the same reality that is expressed by physical objects in *their* relations. Both systems express a single reality; that is to say, "The order and connection of ideas is the same as the order and connection of things" (E-II, 7).

b. Idea and ideatum

We can expand, now, on Spinoza's conception of "idea." From what has been said, it follows that ideas and bodies, as expressions of the same reality, are in some sense identical. An idea is the expression, under the attribute of Thought, of the same reality that a body expresses under the attribute of Extension:

§ . . . a mode of extension and the idea of that mode are one and the same thing expressed in two different ways. (E-II, 7, note)

... *modus extensionis, & idea illius modi una, eademque est res, sed duobus modis expressa.* ...

The terms in this relation between idea and body are called *idea* and *ideatum* by Spinoza. An idea is a mode of Thought, and it is the correlate in Thought of a mode of Extension, its ideatum, which is a physical body. If both attributes are complete, and Spinoza says that they are (E-II, 7, corollary), then every idea must have an ideatum, and vice versa. The ideatum is the object of its idea.[11]

Spinoza uses the relation between idea and ideatum in a number of different ways. Our discussion of attributes has shown that "mental" and "physical" entities should be understood as modes of substance expressed under different attributes. Thus, the distinction between mind and body reduces, for Spinoza, to the distinction between idea and ideatum. The mind and the body are not separate entities; they are different aspects of a single mode of substance. Mind is an aspect of what something is, just as body is an aspect. The same holds for relations between ideas and relations between bodies: they are different aspects of the same thing. Thus, a series of ideas, or modes of Thought, in which each idea is logically entailed by the preceding ideas could be expressed under the attribute of Extension as a series of modes of Extension, each one being *caused* by the preceding members of the series.

[11] "Ideatum" was a scholastic term—"rarement employée," according to Lalande—which referred to something made in accordance with an idea—a work of art, or a product of craftsmanship. In Goclenius it is described as follows: "Ideatum est vi Ideae productum, seu est Ideae effectum," or ". . . ideatum idem est, quod productum est ab Idea." As sources, Goclenius cites Albertus Magnus and Gabriel Biel, and he offers no second definition of the term. The use of "ideatum" in the sense we have been describing in the text, to mean the object of an idea, may be original with Spinoza. Lalande, after describing the usage given in Goclenius, offers the second definition, and Spinoza is the only source cited for it. Eisler defines "ideatum" (*ideat*) as "Vorgestelltes, Gedachtes," but as sources he offers only Goclenius, described above, and Johan Nocolai Tetens, a contemporary of Kant.

Logical relations are, for Spinoza, metaphysically the same as causal relations. We have two different aspects of a single process, not two altogether separate processes or two series of which one could be subordinated to the other. Our account of idea and ideatum is subject to one qualification which is absolutely vital for understanding Spinoza. We have talked so far, for convenience, as if the idea/ideatum distinction coincided with the distinction between Thought and Extension, so that an idea would always be a mode of Thought, and its ideatum a mode of Extension. Often this is the case, but there is no necessity for it to be so. It would be more accurate to say that "idea" and "ideatum" refer to ideas and the things ideas are *of*. If we speak of ideatum as the object of an idea, we must not construe "object" as applying to physical objects only. We can have an idea of a physical object, and when we do, the distinction between idea and ideatum coincides with the distinction between Thought and Extension. But we can have ideas of things that are not physical objects; in particular we can have ideas of ideas. Thus, an idea can have another idea as its ideatum, and when it does both the idea *and* its ideatum are modes of Thought, so that the distinction between idea and ideatum does not coincide with the distinction between Thought and Extension. Failure to recognize that in some cases an idea and its ideatum are both modes of Thought makes it impossible to understand Spinoza's theory of truth; in particular, it makes it impossible to understand how human beings—finite modes—can come to have any true ideas.[12]

Spinoza offers another way of describing the idea/ideatum distinction. He talks of *essentia objectiva* and *essentia formalis*. These expressions—"objective" and "formal"—were fairly well-known in seventeenth-century philosophical litera-

---

[12] Nevertheless, a number of commentators have insisted that the object or ideatum of an idea must be a mode of Extension. For example, see James Martineau, *A Study of Spinoza*, pp. 132 ff.

ture. They are used by Descartes in the third meditation, and perhaps for that reason Spinoza thought that he could presume familiarity with them on the part of his readers. In any case he does not offer detailed explanation. In Descartes "objective reality" refers to the being of a thing as presented or posited by an idea, and "formal reality" refers to the being of the thing itself. In the definitions following the responses to the second set of objections to the *Meditations* he offers the following explanations:

§ Par la *réalité objective d'une idée*, j'entends l'entité ou l'être de la chose représentée par l'idée, en tant que cette entité est dans l'idée . . . Car tout ce que nous concevons comme étant dans les objets des idées, tout cela est objectivement, ou par représentation, dans les idées mêmes. Les mêmes choses sont dites être *formellement* dans les objets des idées, quand elles sont en eux telles que nous les concevons. . . . (ed. Alquié, II, 587; eds. Adam and Tannery, IX, 124–5)

Per realitatem objectivam ideae intelligo entitatem rei repraesentatae per idea, quatenus est in idea . . . Nam quaecumque percipimus tanquam in idearum objectis, ea sunt in ipsis objective. Eadem dicuntur esse formaliter *in idearum objectis, quando talia sunt in ipsis qualia illa percipimus. . . .* (eds. *Adam and Tannery, VII, 161*)

Spinoza takes over this usage, making *essentia objectiva* refer to the being of a thing as it is stated or contained in an idea, and *essentia formalis* refer to the thing in itself—that is, its status in relation to other things of the same kind. Thus, the formal essence of a physical object is its existence *as* a physical object. But physical objects are not the only things that can be said to exist formally; an idea has relations with other ideas—it has a real status *as* an idea—and thus it too can be said to have formal being. As something real an idea I_1 can be thought about, becoming the object of another idea I_2. I_2 is then the idea of an idea (*Idea ideae*), I_1 exists objectively in I_2, which is to say that I_2 contains the objective essence of I_1. This process can be continued indefinitely, since all ideas have *some* real (formal) being. Thus, I_2 can serve as the ideatum of I_3, and I_3 will contain the objective essence of I_2. Spinoza puts this as follows:

§ The idea of a circle is not something having a circumference and a center, as a circle has; nor is the idea of a body that body itself. [That is, the formal being of a circle is not the same as the formal being of the idea of the circle.] Now as it is something different from its correlate, it is capable of being understood through itself; in other words, the idea, in so far as its *essentia formalis* is concerned, may be the object of another *essentia objectiva*. And, again, this second *essentia objectiva* will, regarded in itself, be something real, and capable of being understood; and so on, indefinitely. (*TdIE*, pp. 11–12)

Idea enim circuli non est aliquid, habens peripheriam, & centrum, uti circulus, nec idea corporis est ipsum corpus: & cum sit quid diversum a suo ideato, erit etiam per se aliquid intelligibile; hoc est, idea, quoad suam essentiam formalem, potest esse objectum alterius essentiae objectivae, & rursus haec altera essentia objectiva erit etiam in se spectata quid reale, & intelligibile, & sic indefinite. (II, 14) [13]

Thus, the distinction between *essentia objectiva* and *essentia formalis* is like the distinction between idea and ideatum in that neither distinction always corresponds to the distinction between Thought and Extension.

This usage has distinct advantages for Spinoza. He can speak of the *essentia objectiva* contained in an idea without any commitment as to the formal status of the ideatum, that is, with no commitment as to whether the ideatum exists as a

[13] The notion that an idea has formal reality is also in Descartes, *Meditation III:* ed. Alquié, II, 439 (French), II, 197 (Latin); eds. Adam and Tannery, IX, 32 (French), VII, 41 (Latin).

mode of Extension. The *essentia objectiva* is what is *posited* by the idea; it is like Husserl's "intended meaning" of a concept, and what is "bracketed" by Husserl corresponds to *essentia formalis*.[14] This may be Spinoza's reason for preferring "ideatum" in many passages to the traditional term "object." Since "ideatum" has no meaning except "that which is objectively contained in an idea," one can speak of ideata without prejudicing the question of just what sort of formal reality belongs to them. There need be no connotation—as there could be with "object"—of physical existence.

Since human minds, for Spinoza, are ideas of their bodies (E-II, 10), and since *essentia objectiva* refers to the being of something as contained or posited by an idea, it can happen that *essentia objectiva* refers to the essence of a thing as grasped by a mind; the thing as subjectively apprehended. *Essentia objectiva is* sometimes translated by "subjective essence" (by Elwes, for example).[15] But if we use that rendering we must remember that "subjective" can not retain its present-day connotations of individual bias and fallibility. *Essentia objectiva* is *not* the being of a thing as distorted by a "subjective" interpretation. For what is posited by, say, the definition of a triangle is the same, whoever thinks of the definition. The *essentia objectiva* is given by the *definition* and what the definition says is independent of any individual mind. The *essentia objectiva* contained in an idea is given by the idea itself; whether or not this *essentia objectiva* is a distorted version of the *essentia formalis* of the ideatum is a separate question (which is perhaps prejudged if we translate *objectiva* as "subjective"). But obviously if the idea is a *good* idea of its ideatum, then the reality posited objectively in the

---

[14] This comparison was suggested by Professor Paul O. Kristeller.

[15] In my quotations from Elwes's translation, here and elsewhere, I have replaced "subjective essence" with "*essentia objectiva*," and I have made analogous changes when Spinoza uses the word *objectum* or *objective.*

idea will coincide with the formal reality of the ideatum, and this, I shall later claim, is what Spinoza means by a *true* idea. There remain, however, a number of other problems that must be clarified first.

c. Idea and image

People are frequently hampered, according to Spinoza, in their search for knowledge, by failing to distinguish ideas from images—by confusing intellect and imagination. They suppose that they *understand* something when in fact they only *imagine* it; they think in images—pictures—instead of using ideas alone. In part the distinction between ideas and images corresponds to the distinction between Thought and Extension. Ideas are modifications of Thought, and they are produced by the mind or intellect. Images are modifications of Extension, and products of physical and physiological processes; they come about in so far as the body is affected by other bodies; ". . . the imagination is only affected by physical objects" (*TdIE*, p. 28). The intellect has nothing to do with the formation of images, and the imagination does not, or should not, have any part in the formation of ideas. Sense perception is a physical process, completely dependent on images. Images have their proper use; they can provide some information about other bodies, but they must be carefully distinguished from ideas formed by the mind, and the information they provide must be distinguished from genuine knowledge.

Since images depend on physical relations with other bodies, the information they can provide is fragmentary. We can see, for example, only one side of an object at a time; we can never have the entire object present, at one time, in visual images. Furthermore, since images are produced by the human body in conjunction with an external cause, they reflect the nature of the body as much as the nature of the cause. More accurately, they reflect the body alone, but as modified by some external cause. People with different bodies will have different images of the same things (see E-I, Appendix). Ideas are not subject to these limitations. The order of the intellect is the same for everyone, and if people used their understanding there would be agreement.

§ If men understood things, they (the things) would, as mathematics prove, at least convince all men, if they did not attract them all. (E-I Appendix)

Res enim si intellexissent, illae omnes, teste Mathesi, si non allicerent, ad minimum convincerent.

We can form concepts of things which present the essence of the things as they are. Thus, (1) ideas do not vary for different people, and (2) they can give the full being of the thing. They are not *necessarily* incomplete. Some of our ideas may *be* incomplete, and there may be some kinds of things of which we cannot form complete ideas, but we *could* have complete ideas too. Since knowledge must be valid interpersonally whereas images are different for every person, knowledge can come about only through ideas. Increasing our knowledge means increasing our capacity to understand things and increasing the number of things we actually understand. It does not mean multiplying images.

A further difference between ideas and images lies in the activity or passivity of the mind. Images are formed by the action of other bodies on our body; the body is *acted on* and modified. Ideas, however, are produced by the mind as it thinks; in so far as it is a thinking thing, there is no external force that causes the idea. Thus, the *mind* produces ideas, whereas the imagination depends on causal relations with other bodies. In thinking the mind is active, whereas in imagining it is passive.

§ We know now that the operations, whereby the effects of imagination are produced, take place under other laws quite different from the laws of the understanding, and that the soul is entirely passive with regard to them. (*TdIE*, p. 30)

. . . *novimus operationes illas, a quibus imaginationes producuntur, fieri secundum alias leges, prorsus diversas a legibus intellectus, & animam circa imaginationem tantum habere rationem patientis.* (*II, 32*)

Spinoza emphasizes this point in many places, and it is part of his definition of idea (E-II, def. 3). The distinction between activity and passivity does not apply only to the way ideas and images are produced. There is a difference in the ideas and images themselves. Images are static, like pictures or impressions; ideas are *actions* of the mind. Ideas are not simply the *result* of mental activity, they *are* a kind of mental activity. ". . . an idea, in so far as it is an idea, involves affirmation or negation" (E-II, 49, note).

Despite his frequent insistence on the distinction between ideas and images, Spinoza is not perfectly consistent in his use of the terms, and he occasionally uses "idea" where it would seem that, strictly, he should use "image." This ought not to produce confusion. It is usually clear from the context what he means, and even though he sometimes lapses with "idea" and "image," he does not do so with "intellect" and "imagination." Furthermore, the use of "idea" to indicate both "idea" and "image" as we have defined them was common in the seventeenth century. Descartes, for example, in *Meditation III*, links images and ideas in a way that Spinoza would reject:

§ . . . la lumière naturelle me fait connaître évidemment, que les idées sont en moi comme des tableaux, ou des images. . . . (ed. Alquié, II, 440; eds. Adam and Tannery, IX, 33)

Adeo ut lumine naturali mihi sit perspicuum ideas in me esse veluti quasdam imagines. . . . (*ed. Alquié, II, 197; eds. Adam & Tannery, VII, 42*)

Many writers used "idea" indiscriminately to mean both "concept" and "percept," and in separating the two Spinoza was going against the ordinary usage.[16] Sometimes Spinoza's use of "idea" for "image" may be a case of his using the word according to the ordinary usage of the day, where he did not think that his meaning would be obscured.

But the terminological confusion is not always a case of using "idea" where "image" seems to be required. A better account, in some cases, would be to say that there are two kinds of ideas: those derived from images and those not derived from images. We have remarked that images can provide limited information about other bodies. Such information can be systematized; ideas derived from images in the body are used to make inferences and to guide our actions. Most of our daily life, in fact, is conducted on this level (the "first kind of knowledge"). But for philosophical purposes, ideas formed from images must be kept separate from pure ideas—those produced by the mind alone, without any reliance on images. A common source of error, in Spinoza's opinion, is the supposition that images can provide the basis for rational understanding. Empirical knowledge is useful, even indispensable, but it is not *understanding*.

d. Rational explanation, knowledge, and determinism

If empirical knowledge does not give understanding, then what does? To ask this is to ask what, for Spinoza, constitutes an explanation.[17] Spinoza does not use the word "explanation." He talks of "understanding" things, or of "knowing their causes." To ask what is Spinoza's concept of rational explanation is much the same as asking "what does Spinoza say it means to 'understand' something?" But I do not think it is

---

[16] J. O. Urmson, article "Ideas," p. 119.

[17] A fuller account of Spinoza's conception of explanation, in substantial agreement with the one offered here, may be found in Hampshire, *Spinoza*, pp. 29–36.

misleading to use the word "explanation," and there will be other times when I shall deliberately use terminology that Spinoza did not use. I believe that in this way his doctrines can be made clearer to us.

In the first place, anything that can count as an explanation for Spinoza is *rational,* not emotional, or rhetorical, or merely persuasive. Spinoza could put this by saying that an explanation appeals to the intellect alone, and not to imagination or desire. Reasoning, for Spinoza, means deduction; to give a rational explanation means to present a deductive argument. The explanation of "p" is a deductive argument with self-evident premises and "p" as its conclusion. An explanation of this kind would be described as giving the *cause* of what it explains; we have seen that for Spinoza logical relations and causal relations come to the same thing. The cause of something is its logically necessary and sufficient condition. This is sometimes expressed by saying that for Spinoza "cause" means formal cause alone.[18] Given his conception of "cause," it makes sense for Spinoza to look for the cause of many things that we might think do not lend themselves to causal explanation. His ideas were novel in his own time, as he recognized; witness his defense, in the preface to Part III of the *Ethics,* of his use of the same kind of explanation in discussing human emotions as he used in discussing God.

But even in cases where we might today deny the appropriateness of a causal explanation, we may nevertheless grant that *some* explanation is in order. We talk, for instance, of historical explanation, and some writers maintain that a different model of explanation is involved here than we have in

---

[18] " 'Cause' for Spinoza means, not force, not mechanical or efficient cause, but that in terms of which a thing is intelligible—its logical ground, its *arche,* its principle of intelligibility. Although Spinoza characteristically refuses to define this basic concept, it is clear that to him 'cause' is always to be identified with formal cause alone" (John H. Randall, Jr., *The Career of Philosophy* I, p. 439).

physics.[19] Spinoza does not admit different kinds of explanation: anything that is to count as an explanation must be a deductive argument such as we have described. What this amounts to is an insistence on the uniformity of nature and the unity of science. Such a view may, to some extent, underlie any philosophic or scientific inquiry, but in Spinoza it is pushed to its extreme limit. All things, he says, can be explained according to a single conception of explanation, and there is no need for different modes of explanation. The same model of explanation applies to any inquiry we undertake. Nature

§ . . . is always the same and everywhere one. Her force is the same, and her power of acting, that is to say, her laws and rules, according to which all things occur and are changed from form to form, are everywhere and always the same, so that there must also be one and the same method of understanding the nature of all things whatsoever, that is to say, by the universal laws and rules of Nature. (E-III, preface)

. . . *est namque natura semper eadem, & ubique una, eademque ejus virtus, & agendi potentia, hoc est, naturae leges, & regulae, secundum quas omnia fiunt, & ex unis formis in alias mutantur, sunt ubique, & semper eaedem, atque adeo una, eademque etiam debet esse ratio rerum qualiumcunque naturam intelligendi, nempe per leges, & regulas naturae universales.*

In saying that any explanation must take a particular form, Spinoza is not just saying that if there is to be explanation it must be of the kind we have described. For that leaves the possibility of things that cannot be explained at all. Spinoza is not saying that those things that can be explained must be explained according to his model, but not all things can be

---

[19] See, for instance, William Dray, *Laws and Explanation in History.*

explained. He takes a stronger position: not only are all explanations of the same kind, but also anything whatever can be explained. That is, he believes that anything at all can be presented as the logical conclusion of a deductive argument proceeding from self-evident premises. We have two points here which are absolutely essential in Spinoza's philosophy: (1) there is a *single* scheme of explanation. The logical form of whatever is to count as an explanation can be specified once for all, and there are no special kinds of things that require special kinds of explanation; (2) *everything* can be explained. We may—and we do, as a matter of fact—have satisfactory explanations of very few things, but there is nothing of which it is impossible in principle to give an explanation. There are no a priori limits to knowledge. This appears to contradict the claim that empirical knowledge necessarily falls short of genuine understanding. But the deficiency of our understanding of extended nature comes about because of our status as finite modes, not because extended nature is ordered in some way that makes explanation impossible.

The doctrine that everything can be explained is one way of expressing Spinoza's determinism, since it amounts to the claim that everything has a cause, taking "cause" in Spinoza's sense. There can be no event without a cause, for if something had no cause it could not be understood—that is, it could not be given an explanation. The claim that everything can be explained is thus equivalent to the claim that there is nothing without a cause. And if "determinism" means that no events are free—uncaused—then Spinoza is a determinist.[20]

But this kind of determinism should be distinguished from other forms of determinism. Spinoza's view could be called a "rationalist determinism," based on the rationalist's belief in the possibility of rational explanation. It may be that deter-

---

[20] Spinoza's determinism is well discussed by Hampshire in "Spinoza and the Idea of Freedom." See especially pp. 208 f.

minism always involves—or even consists in—such a claim;
the claim, that is, that everything can be explained according
to a particular model of explanation. If so, it is important to
keep separate the different models of explanation that can be
offered. Spinoza's determinism should not be confused with,
say, a mechanistic determinism—that is, with the claim that
everything can be explained according to the laws of mechanics. For even if Spinoza admitted (as, in fact, he does)
that the laws of mechanics could explain all physical events
—that is, if the laws of mechanics could account for all modifications of Extension—that would still be an account of substance under only one of its infinite attributes. Thus, although
Spinoza might accept mechanics as a means of explaining Extension, he would not say that all explanation was
mechanistic explanation. Therefore, Spinoza's determinism is
not mechanistic determinism. Roth writes that "To Spinoza
the mechanistic account of things, although valid, is not complete. It is true within its sphere. . . ." [21]

Spinoza's conception of knowledge follows directly from
what has been said. Knowing something means having an explanation of it, which is the same thing as knowing its cause.
"The knowledge of an effect is nothing else than the acquisition of more perfect knowledge of its cause" (*TdIE*, p. 31). I
know if I can give a deduction from self-evident premises
with the thing to be known as the conclusion. Since there is
nothing that cannot be explained, there is nothing that is
unknowable in principle. It follows also that knowledge is
certain. For if the premises *are* self-evident, and the deduction is correct, there can be no room for doubt. Questions
may still come up: *when* are the premises "self-evident," and
how do we know this? Spinoza's answers to these questions
are provided by his theory of truth itself, which I take up in
the next chapter.

[21] *Spinoza*, p. 84.

The three conceptions we have just discussed—rational explanation, determinism, and knowledge—are very closely related. If there is to be knowledge in Spinoza's sense, then determinism, in the sense given above, is required. To deny determinism would be to deny the possibility of rational explanation, which would be to rule out knowledge. Something that is not determined—which cannot be explained—cannot be known. There may, of course, be things that we do not know; it turns out, in fact, that there are a great many things that we cannot explain. Indeed we might wonder whether there is *anything* that we can plausibly claim to know in Spinoza's strict sense of knowing. Spinoza admits that our knowledge is limited, but he insists that we do have *some* knowledge, even in the strict sense. Just what things he believes that we know will emerge in subsequent discussion. The point so far has been to indicate Spinoza's ideal and his general orientation.

III. The definition of truth

SPINOZA'S MOST EXPLICIT discussions of truth are in the *TdIE* and in the *Ethics*.[1] In the *TdIE*, Spinoza presents his views as if to someone just beginning his studies, whereas in the *Ethics* he follows what he considers the proper intellectual order. Accordingly, although the most concise and authoritative formulation of Spinoza's conclusions

---

[1] The precise purpose of the *TdIE* and its relation to the *Ethics* are not known. Commentators have claimed that *TdIE* was intended as an introduction to a larger work which Spinoza never wrote, that Spinoza abandoned it in favor of the *Ethics,* that it was to serve as an introduction to the *Ethics* itself, that it was given up because of internal philosophic difficulties—but the fact is that we do not have enough information to decide with certainty which of these is correct. See Carl Gebhardt, *Spinozas Abhandlung über die Verbesserung des Verstandes;* also Harold H. Joachim, *Spinoza's Tractatus de Intellectus Emendatione,* Chapter I. Their results are discussed and compared by David Bidney, "Joachim on Spinoza's Tractatus de Intellectus Emendatione," pp. 47–55.

is in the *Ethics,* some doctrines which are given fairly brief treatment in the *Ethics* are stated more fully in the *TdIE,* where Spinoza is concerned to persuade as well as to demonstrate. In the *TdIE* we find supporting material that would be hard to reconstruct from the *Ethics* alone. Consequently, in an attempt to provide some of the considerations that can lead to a position like Spinoza's, I shall at first adopt an order of presentation closer to the *TdIE* than to the *Ethics.*

In the *TdIE,* as in the *Ethics,* Spinoza's ultimate concern is the question "What is the supreme good for man?" The discussion of true ideas comes up in the course of attacking this fundamental question. After listing some of the investigations that would be required for a complete knowledge of human nature and of man's highest perfection, Spinoza raises questions about knowledge itself, since before we can proceed to other investigations we must know how to recognize knowledge.

a. Criterion of truth

At the beginning of any inquiry, a methodologically self-conscious person might ask, "How would I recognize the truth if I found it?" This question has a long history, and it can be given a paradoxical formulation, as in Plato's *Meno:* "A man cannot inquire either about that which he knows or about that which he does not know; for if he knows, he has no need to inquire; and if not, he cannot; for he does not know the very subject about which he is to inquire" (80e). Inquiry is thus unnecessary or impossible. If we reject this paradoxical formulation, and try instead to provide criteria of truth that do not presuppose the results of our inquiry or rule out inquiry altogether, then there is danger of an infinite regress. (For if we say that truth can always be recognized by a certain sign "S" then someone can always ask me how I *know* that S is a sign of truth; if I say "because S has property *R*," the same question comes up about R, and so on.) Thus, in specifying the procedure we are to follow ". . . we must first take care not to commit ourselves to a search, going back to infinity—that is, in order to discover the best method for finding out the truth, there is no need of another method to discover such method; nor of a third method for discovering the second, and so on to infinity. By such proceedings, we should never arrive at the knowledge of the truth, or, indeed, at any knowledge at all" (*TdIE*, pp. 10–11). A requirement, therefore, of a theory of truth, or of a method of investigation, is that it enable us to answer the question "how do you know?" in some way that does not lead to an infinite regress.[2]

One way to avoid the infinite regress would be to say that a starting point must be accepted without proof. Not *every-thing* can be explained, so we must accept some things without explanation, as axioms or as definitions. The only way to avoid an infinite regress is to refuse to embark on it, and looking for guarantees or necessary and sufficient conditions before setting out is precisely to embark on an infinite regress. This solution of the difficulty is frequently accepted. Notice, however, that if we accept it we will not be entitled to claim that our premises are *true*. The best we will be able to do is to say that they are consistent, or economical, or that various consequences follow if we adopt them, and *these* considerations, rather than their truth, will be offered as reasons for adopting the premises. This limitation is accepted with equanimity by many logicians today, but Spinoza would not have accepted it. He maintained that some things *were* true, and could be known with certainty to be true. To accept something on pragmatic grounds, or merely because we have to start somewhere, would be irrational.

Besides being irrational in Spinoza's view, this solution

---

[2] The infinite regress plays an important part in the discussion of the criterion of truth in Sextus Empiricus, *Outlines of Pyrrhonism*, Book II, Chapter 9, and elsewhere; and Spinoza's arguments may have been directed against Sextus or those influenced by him.

would not really solve anything. It would mean abandoning *all* our claims to certain knowledge, not only the claim that our premises are true. For we cannot claim that our conclusion must be true if we have abandoned the claim that the premises are true. Perhaps we could say that *if* the premises are true, *then* the conclusion is true too—surely that much we can accept. But how do we know that? Perhaps because the conclusion was reached according to specifiable rules of inference? What guarantee is there that the rules will always produce correct results? I can offer a proof that my rules of inference cannot give false conclusions from true premises—but the same question can then be asked about the proof as about the rules. Giving up our pretensions, therefore, about the truth of particular statements—the premises—does not avoid the infinite regress.

There is a further difficulty. Suppose that we have a set of premises which we know to be true, and a set of rules such that if the premises are true any conclusion obtained according to the rules must be true too. There could still be questions about the applications of the rules. How can I be sure that a given inference is one of the kind justified by the rules? How do I know that a given statement is an instance of something described by my rules? Perhaps I need a second set of rules, telling me, for each combination of premises, which of the first rules can be applied. We are involved again in an infinite regress. It appears that we must give up all claims whatever to truth, since we can give no guarantee that is not itself subject to question.

The infinite regress was generated by the search for an external criterion of truth—one that could be specified in advance and could be known in advance to be reliable. Spinoza would reject the solution suggested above, that we simply accept something "by convention" or "by definition," without any guarantee. He does not discuss this alternative himself; I have brought it in because it is one that has been commonly accepted in recent times. But since the proposed solution involves abandoning the claim that we can know anything with perfect certainty, it is clear that Spinoza would reject it. Rather than give up the possibility of certain knowledge, Spinoza gives up the search for an external criterion:

§ Thus, as the truth needs no sign . . . it follows that the true method does not consist in seeking for the signs of truth after the acquisition of the idea. . . . (*TdIE*, p. 13)

Cum itaque veritas nullo egeat signo, . . . hinc sequitur, quod vera non est Methodus signum veritatis quaerere post acquisitionem idearum. . . . (II, 15)

Some things, he says, can be known to be true without any external guarantee. Truth, in Spinoza's phrase, is its own criterion:

§ What can be clearer or more certain than a true idea as a standard of truth? Just as light reveals both itself and the darkness, so truth is the standard of itself and of the false. (E-II, 43, note)

Deinde quid idea vera clarius, & certius dari potest, quod norma sit veritatis? Sane sicut lux seipsam, & tenebras manifestat, sic veritas norma sui, & falsi est.

This claim does not, perhaps, seem especially plausible. But then, it is easily misunderstood. To appreciate Spinoza's position, we must call to mind the conception of "idea" mentioned earlier (pp. 23 f). Spinoza is talking about ideas, not images; ideas in which the mind is active. Ideas are acts of the mind, not static impressions or "dumb pictures." Spinoza says that

§ . . . an idea, in so far as it is an idea, involves affirmation or negation. (E-II, 49, note. See also E-II, 48, with its note, and proposition 49 itself.)

. . . non vident, ideam, quatenus idea est, affirmationem, aut negationem involvere.

A true idea is not so much like an image as it is like a true statement, or better, a valid inference. When he says that truth is its own criterion, Spinoza is saying that the truth of an inference is revealed by understanding the inference; once we understand it, no other proof is required, and no other proof is possible which will not itself require justification—the infinite regress again—or else rest on the same sort of understanding. In either case, truth is revealed and guaranteed by understanding alone.

If we do not understand an inference and ask for an explanation, the only possible explanation is that we should go over the inference again, think about it, and try to understand it. Thus, either I know that from "A implies B" along with "A is true" it is valid to infer "B is true," in which case it is silly to ask why the inference is true, or I don't know that it is valid, in which case I don't understand it. (For convenience, I shall henceforth refer to this inference—the traditional principle called *modus ponens*—in logical symbols, thus:"A ⊃ B.A. ⊃ B.") The only way to know that an inference is true is to understand it. Understanding is a necessary and sufficient condition for knowing truth. This is what Spinoza means by saying that truth is its own criterion. If someone has never had a true idea, he cannot possibly know what it would be like to have one. The only way to understand truth is to have—to understand—a true idea (understanding is a *necessary* condition). Conversely, if we understand something we cannot refuse to accept it. We cannot agree or disagree at will (understanding is a *sufficient* condition).

I cannot understand "A ⊃ B.A. ⊃ B" and still say that I'm not sure whether it's true or not. We can, of course, remember how things seemed before we reached our present level of understanding, and we can talk as if we didn't understand, or suppose something that we know to be false—in a proof, say, for a *reductio ad absurdum* argument. But once we have understood "A ⊃ B.A. ⊃ B" we cannot *know* its negation—

"A ⊃ B.A. ⊃ ∼ B"—although we could use it in an argument; showing, say, that it implies "B and not-B" ("B.∼ B") which is absurd. This is the point of Spinoza's discussion of "feigning," where he says that we are not free to make fictions about eternal truths. (*TdIE*, pp. 17–21; *Opera*, II, 19–24). He is not talking—as he has been understood to talk—about the kinds of grammatical structure that could follow the word "suppose." [3] He agrees that we can follow the word "suppose" by any other words we like, but then, "many things we can affirm and deny, because the nature of words allows us to do so, though the nature of things does not" (*TdIE*, p. 30).

b. Method

Once a person has a true idea, it can be used as a model for other ideas, and as a guide in searching for additional knowledge. Spinoza's example of the hammer is relevant here (*TdIE*, p. 11; *Opera*, II, 13). He talks of the argument purporting to show that people cannot use iron. For to work iron we need a hammer, but a hammer is made of iron, so to make a hammer we must first be able to work iron—but to work iron we need a hammer, and so on. One point of that example is to illustrate the infinite regress discussed above; Spinoza says that in looking for a guarantee of truth we must beware of a search that goes to infinity. But he also points out that one use of tools is to make better tools: starting with crude instruments we produce better ones, and the new instruments can be used to produce still better ones. The case, he says, is the same with true ideas. We begin with a true idea, which serves both as a model for evaluating other ideas and as information that can lead to a more adequate understanding.

[3] "It might be thought that any kind of statement can follow the words 'Suppose that . . .'; but Spinoza asserts that this is not so" (G. H. R. Parkinson, *Spinoza's Theory of Knowledge*, p. 98).

§ The intellect, by its native strength, makes for itself intellectual instruments, whereby it acquires strength for performing other intellectual operations. . . . (*TdIE*, p. 11)

. . . *intellectus vi sua nativa facit sibi instrumenta intellectualia, quibus alias vires acquirit ad alia opera intellectualia. (II, 14).*

Method, for Spinoza, consists in understanding a true idea. The question posed at the outset—how can we acquire knowledge, and how can we be sure that what we discover is true?—is answered by saying that first we must understand a true idea (and the only way to understand it is to *have* it and to think about it). Then we can evaluate other ideas by using this one as a model, and we can gain new information and better understanding by using this idea to develop other ideas. In this way, we can gradually build an intricate structure of knowledge. Spinoza is perfectly explicit about all this:

§ Method is not identical with reasoning in the search for causes, still less is it the comprehension of the causes of things: it is the understanding of what a true idea is. . . . (*TdIE*, p. 13)

. . . *Methodus non est ipsum ratiocinari ad intelligendum causas rerum, & multa minus est τὸ intelligere causas rerum; sed est intelligere, quid sit vera idea. (II, 15)*

§ . . . in proportion as it acquires new ideas, the mind simultaneously acquires new instruments for pursuing its inquiries further. (*TdIE*, p. 13)

. . . *mens, plura intelligendo, alia simul acquirat instrumenta, quibus facilius pergat intelligere. (II, 16).*

§ Again, the more things the mind knows, the better does it understand its own strength and the order of Nature; by increased self-knowledge it can direct itself more easily, and lay down rules for its own guidance; . . . (*TdIE*, p. 14)

Deinde, quo plura mens novit, eo melius & suas vires, &

ordinem Naturae intelligit: quo autem melius suas vires intel-
ligit, eo facilius potest seipsam dirigere, & regulas sibi pro-
ponere. (*II, 16*)

I have insisted on the role played by the true idea partly in order to dispel a common misunderstanding. Spinoza is not setting up an a priori science, in which we would establish a number of true ideas—or one true idea—and proceed to *deduce* everything else that we wanted to know. On the contrary, his procedure has features in common with Descartes's *cogito ergo sum,* and both of them have at times been misunderstood. Descartes's *cogito* has been taken as a premiss, from which Descartes proposed to deduce everything else. It is generally agreed now, however, that Descartes is offering a model of a clear and distinct idea, rather than a premiss, and saying that other ideas can be *evaluated* by comparison with this one, although they may not be *deducible* from it. Spinoza is doing a similar thing. He is saying that in order to recognize true ideas we must know what a true idea is like, and the only way to know what a true idea is like is to have one.

To say that Spinoza proposes a deductive program of scientific investigation is to confuse his method with his ideal of explanation. An acceptable explanation for him *is* a deductive structure, one in which what is to be explained appears as the deductive consequence of self-evident premisses—an explanatory model that has been accepted by many writers. We know, after the discussion above, something more about what Spinoza means by "self-evident premisses." Spinoza also believed that complete knowledge of the universe, once attained, could be presented in a *single* deductive system. This position is related to his view, discussed earlier (above, p. 29), that anything whatever can be given an explanation, or has a cause. Many people would deny the possibility of a single all-encompassing deductive explanatory system, even if they accepted Spinoza's conception of explanation. But de-

spite his belief in the unity of science—if that is what his belief comes to—Spinoza did not believe that we, human beings
with finite minds, should try to investigate nature by deduction. The point becomes clearer if we point out that "method"
for Spinoza refers to the way of evaluating our knowledge, or
of critically assessing whatever is put forward as explanation.
"Method" does not mean the *procedure*—the concrete steps
for making new discoveries. It is worth repeating a passage
already quoted: "Method is not identical with reasoning in
the search for causes. . . ." (*TdIE*, p. 13) We often take
"method" to mean a concrete program of investigation—a
logic of scientific discovery—but that is not what Spinoza
meant by it. Since he is discussing method in his sense, and
not giving us a blueprint for inquiry, Spinoza gives us only
the merest hint about inquiry. His position might have been
less misunderstood if he had not been so careful to leave out
anything that was not strictly relevant to his discussion. But
he admits explicitly that a concrete investigation requires a
procedure different from the method he has been discussing
here; "other aids," he says, are necessary, although, in line
with his general conciseness, he does not permit himself to digress. However, in view of the common misunderstanding of
Spinoza's views, the passage is worth quoting at some length.
In order to understand particular mutable things,

§ Other aids are therefore needed besides those employed for
understanding eternal things and their laws; however, this is
not the place to recount such aids, nor is there any need to
do so, until we have acquired a sufficient knowledge of eternal things and their infallible laws, and until the nature of
our senses has become plain to us.

Before betaking ourselves to seek knowledge of particular
things, it will be seasonable to speak of such aids, as all tend
to teach us the mode of employing our senses, and to make
certain experiments under fixed rules and arrangement which
may suffice to determine the object of our inquiry, so that we

may therefrom infer what laws of eternal things it has been produced under, and may gain an insight into its inmost nature, as I will duly show. Here, to return to my purpose, I will only endeavor to set forth what seems necessary for enabling us to attain to knowledge of eternal things, and to define them under the conditions laid down above (*TdIE*, pp. 34–35)

Unde alia auxilia necessario sunt quaerenda praeter illa, quibus utimur ad res aeternas, earumque leges intelligendum; attamen non est hujus loci ea tradere, neque etiam opus est, nisi postquam rerum aeternarum, earumque infallibilium legum sufficientem acquisiverimus cognitionem, sensuumque nostrorum natura nobis innotuerit.

Antequam ad rerum singularium cognitionem accingamur, tempus erit, ut ea auxilia tradamus, quae omnia eo tendent, ut nostris sensibus sciamus uti, & experimenta certis legibus, & ordine facere, quae sufficient ad rem, quae inquiritur, determinandam, ut tandem ex iis concludamus, secundum quasnam rerum aeternarum leges facta sit, & intima ejus natura nobis innotescat, ut suo loco ostendam. Hic, ut ad propositum revertar, tantum enitar tradere, quae videntur necessaria, ut ad cognitionem rerum aeternarum pervenire possimus, earumque definitiones formemus conditionibus supra traditis. (*II*, 37)

Although he does not recommend that we try to deduce statements of fact, Spinoza's ideal of explanation *is* a deductive one. And, to the extent that we have adequate explanations of anything, the true ideas we have discussed will be premisses in deductive arguments. *Complete* knowledge *would* be a deductive system:

§ . . . in order to reproduce in every respect the faithful image of Nature, our mind must deduce all its ideas from the idea which represents the origin and source of the whole of Nature. . . . (*TdIE*, p. 14)

. . . *ut mens nostra omnino referat Naturae exemplar, de-*

beat omnes suas ideas producere ab ea, quae refert originem,
& fontem totius Naturae, . . . (*II, 17*)

This claim of Spinoza's seems to me very like the famous remark of Laplace, to the effect that if given a complete set of
laws and of initial conditions, an infinite intelligence could
deduce all states of the universe. It happens, of course, that
we do not know all the laws and initial conditions, and we
do not possess infinite intelligence. Spinoza would admit this
as readily as Laplace. Our minds cannot, in fact, "reproduce
in every respect the faithful image of Nature." But Spinoza
does not believe that this impossibility vitiates his conception
of what a complete explanation would be like. And it remains
true that *if* ". . . by some happy chance anyone had adopted
this method in his investigations of Nature—that is, if he had
acquired new ideas in the proper order, according to the
standard of the original true idea, he would never have
doubted of the truth of his knowledge, inasmuch as truth, as
we have seen, makes itself manifest, and all things would
flow, as it were, spontaneously to him" (*TdIE*, p. 15). Nevertheless, the "conditions of human life," among other things,
prevent anyone from actually proceeding in this way.[4]

We may now sum up this part of our discussion. Spinoza's
concept of explanation was deductive, and he believed that
the universe was rational, so that it could, in principle, be
represented as a gigantic system in which every part would
be logically implied by the other parts. But he did not believe that human intelligence could proceed by deduction
alone in its investigation of nature. We can know some things
with certainty, but we cannot proceed exclusively according

---

[4] The notion that Spinoza believed in a deductive investigation of
matters of fact may seem obvious nonsense, but it is found in a great
many commentators. It appears, for example, in James Martineau, *A
Study of Spinoza*, p. 125, and, more recently, in G. H. R. Parkinson,
Spinoza's Theory of Knowledge, Chapter 2.

to the order of the intellect. A finite intelligence like ours must rely on "other aids" as well. Without claiming anything stronger than coincidence, we may point out that Spinoza here is close to Aristotle's view that what is most knowable in itself is often least knowable to us, and we must begin with what is knowable to us and proceed to what is knowable in itself.

At this point, someone might make the following objection: "Do we have any true ideas? I agree that if we have, then we can proceed as you say, and use our true ideas as models for other ideas, thereby increasing our knowledge. But you still have to show that we have at least one true idea." I am not convinced that this objection is consistent with an understanding of Spinoza's argument. It seems to me that if one did understand Spinoza's claim about the nature of true ideas and the need for avoiding an infinite regress, then this understanding itself would be a true idea of the sort required, and it would not be reasonable to go on to ask whether we have any true ideas. For Spinoza's argument has been: "If you understand what a true idea is, that is all you need; and the only way to understand a true idea is to have one." According to that argument it would be nonsense to say "I understand what you mean by 'true idea,' and all I need to know is whether I have any ideas like that," since having a true idea is both necessary and sufficient for understanding "true idea." It would be self-contradictory for someone both to understand what a true idea is and to doubt whether he has one.

Neverthless, Spinoza takes the trouble to show that we do have true ideas. This may be partly to satisfy the invalid objection just discussed. The person making it does not understand (or he would not make the objection), but perhaps he can be made to understand if we treat him politely and discuss his question. It would be characteristic of Spinoza to take such an attitude (witness his letters to Boxel). But Spinoza's demonstration that we do have true ideas has philosophic importance as well, which will perhaps emerge best if we treat it in connection with the question of the coherence theory of truth.

c. Coherence theory: some difficulties

Many writers say, as if it were an obvious fact, that Spinoza held a coherence theory of truth.[5] According to the coherence theory, the truth of an idea is ascertained only by its relations to other ideas, and it is claimed that an isolated idea cannot be said to be true. This view of truth differs from the one I have been presenting as Spinoza's, and it has the distinct disadvantage of being explicitly contradicted by him:

§ . . . the form of true thought must exist in the thought itself, without reference to other thoughts; . . . (*TdIE*, p. 24)

. . . *forma verae cogitationis in eadem ipsa cogitatione sine relatione ad alias debet esse sita;* . . . (*II, 26–27*)

---

[5] "If, in Spinoza's view, a proposition is to be true and certain, its truth and certainty can be exhibited only when that proposition is shown to be a part of a total deductive system of such propositions, the truth of each of which depends on its connection with all the others" (Alasdair MacIntyre, article "Spinoza," p. 532). ". . . the argument [that truth is its own criterion] leads inevitably to what is a central tenet of his logic —namely, to a qualified form of what is called the coherence theory of truth" (Stuart Hampshire, *Spinoza*, p. 76). "The criterion of truth, as of reality, lies in coherence within the self-inclusive whole" (Leon Roth, *Spinoza*, p. 27). See also H. H. Joachim, *Study*, pp. 148 f.
Although many commentators have described Spinoza as a coherence theorist, not *all* have done so. H. F. Hallett, for example, offers a different view, emphasizing "what is central in Spinoza's theory, viz. the intrinsic *agency* of ideas" (*Benedict de Spinoza*, p. 60). I agree that possession of true ideas is *action* of the mind (see Chapter V, below), but it seems to me that Hallett does not give sufficient weight to Axiom 6, Pt. I (quoted below, p. 51), which, as we shall see, Spinoza treats as a definition of truth. A very different interpretation, making extensive use of the terminology and literature of analytic philosophy, is offered by E. M. Curley (*Spinoza's Metaphysics*, pp. 122–26). Curley interprets the agreement of idea and ideatum in terms of an agreement of facts and the propositions which express them.

In particular, Spinoza's argument about the infinite regress, and his subsequent claim that truth is its own criterion go against the coherence view. For, according to the coherence theory, if we wish to determine whether an idea is true we must examine its relations with other ideas. Spinoza has been at pains to say that such a procedure leads to an infinite regress. A coherence theorist may agree, and say that the infinite regress simply proves that no idea can be known to be true apart from all other ideas. But Spinoza has refused to accept any theory that led to an infinite regress. Furthermore, Spinoza's doctrine of truth as its own criterion shows that for him a true idea *can* be understood by itself; it is the nature of the idea or act of the mind that reveals its truth, not its relations to other ideas. Spinoza insists frequently that truth is revealed by the intrinsic nature of an idea.

I have pointed out that coherence as commonly formulated is not Spinoza's criterion of truth, but it might be that coherence could serve as a definition even if it were not a criterion. This does not seem especially plausible if, as Spinoza says, truth is the criterion of itself. For it would not be reasonable (1) to define truth as coherence, and (2) to say that it is the criterion of itself, and at the same time (3) to say that a true idea is not recognized by its relations with other ideas. Any two of these statements may be compatible, but the conjunction of all three is inconsistent. Spinoza does explicitly assert (2) and (3), which we have quoted above. Since he nowhere asserts (1), and since (1) is inconsistent with the things he does say explicitly, we would need special justification for attributing (1) to him. This rejection of the coherence view follows logically only if "coherence" is taken to mean a certain kind of interrelation between ideas, for only if we take it that way is (1) inconsistent with the conjunction of (2) and (3). But since coherence usually *is* taken that way, we have at least shown that Spinoza does not hold the coherence theory as commonly formulated.

Despite the objections I have offered to a coherence theory of truth in Spinoza, there are features of his philosophy that can be used to support it. His ideal of explanation, as we have seen, was a deductive arrangement, in which every statement or idea to be explained would follow logically from the other parts of the system. He believed, further, that the universe was in fact arranged so that all parts of it are causally related to other parts; thus we could not give part of it a complete causal explanation without understanding the whole. From this, would it not follow that we cannot fully know anything? If a true idea is revealed by understanding, and if understanding means understanding the whole, would it not follow that only the idea of the whole can be true? That the only idea which contains its own criterion is the idea of the whole? Thus, according to Spinoza's own theory of explanation and his own doctrine that truth is its own criterion, it would follow that nothing can be understood except in relation to the whole, and since it could not be understood it could not be known to be true.

We have arrived at two positions that are commonly associated with the coherence theory: (1) the view that the only perfectly true idea is the idea of the whole and that no idea less than the whole can be perfectly true, and (2) the doctrine, usually derived from the preceding, of degrees of truth, according to which all ideas less than the idea of the whole are only "more or less" true. Since Spinoza's theory of explanation, and his belief in a rationally ordered universe, seem to lead to these positions, it may be reasonable to attribute to him a coherence theory of truth. If we wish to reject that consequence, some special argument is required.

Spinoza's demonstration that we do have true ideas is precisely that argument. He needs to show how it can happen that despite the conception of explanation and the interconnection of things, a finite intellect can have true ideas. His concept of method clearly depends on the possibility of a

finite intellect having true ideas; the entire exposition of the
TdIE, in which he claims that to recognize truth we must first
have a true idea, would be undermined if his metaphysics
made it impossible for us to have any true ideas at all.

He argues that if there is anything that is present equally
in the part and in the whole, then it can be understood
through the part as well as through the whole:

§ Those things which are common to everything, and which
are equally in the part and in the whole, can only be adequately conceived. (E-II, 38)

*Illa, quae omnibus communia, quaeque aeque in parte, ac
in toto sunt, non possunt concipi, nisi adaequate.*

The idea of God is present everywhere, since in forming the
idea of any particular object we must consider its relations
with other objects and we are led to conceive, as the logical
limit of this procedure, the self-sufficient system of intercon-
nected things. Thus,

§ Every idea of any body or actually existing individual
thing necessarily involves the eternal and infinite essence of
God. (E-II, 45)

*Unaquaeque cujuscunque corporis, vel rei singularis, actu
existentis, idea Dei aeternam, & infinitam essentiam necessario involvit.*

If the idea of God is common to everything, it follows by
Proposition 38 that it must be an adequate idea, or

§ The knowledge of the eternal and infinite essence of God
which each idea involves is adequate and perfect. (E-II, 46)

*Cognitio aeternae, & infinitae essentiae Dei, quam una-
quaeque idea involvit, est adaequata, & perfecta.*

Here we have the true idea that Spinoza's method requires.
We can use that true idea as a guide and as a model (not as
a premiss) and acquire other true ideas, thus enlarging our

knowledge. This conclusion fits at least that part of the coherence view that says that only the idea of the whole is true. But Spinoza's belief that we have adequate knowledge of the whole would not appeal to many coherence theorists.

If the idea of God is the true idea that we have, this may raise questions about the example used in the exposition of Spinoza's concept of true idea. Inferences like "A ⊃ B.A. ⊃ B" are not God, but only laws of logic. However, these inferences *are* present in the part as well as in the whole, even though they are confined to a single attribute. The laws of logic apply throughout the attribute of thought; all thoughts are equally subject to them, and any thoughts can be used to illustrate them. They are, therefore, common to everything, equally in the part and in the whole, and they can only be adequately conceived. Perhaps we could say that there are two kinds of true idea: (1) the idea of God and (2) ideas that are common to everything (such as the laws of logic, or, in extension, of geometry). But this separation seems artificial, and I am not sure that it can be supported from Spinoza's writings.

Now, anything that gives knowledge of God is common to all:

§ . . . that which gives a knowledge of the eternal and infinite essence of God is common to all, and is equally in the part and in the whole. (E-II, 46, dem.)

. . . *id, quod cognitionem aeternae, & infinitae essentiae Dei dat, omnibus commune, & aeque in parte, ac in toto est* . . . .

If we could show that the converse of this holds also—that whatever is common to all and is equally present in the part and in the whole gives knowledge of the eternal and infinite essence of God—then we could say that the two kinds of true ideas suggested above are really the same. This would amount to saying that any true idea is fundamentally the idea of God or substance. I think that this can be done; and I further think that the relationship between truth and substance is the heart of Spinoza's theory of truth. But this can best be brought out after we have clarified Spinoza's definition of truth, so I shall postpone it until the next chapter.

d. Correspondence theory: some difficulties

The statement of Spinoza that most resembles a formal definition of truth is in Part I of the *Ethics:*

§ A true idea must agree with that of which it is the idea. (Axiom 6)

Idea vera debet cum suo ideato convenire.

This sounds like a correspondence definition of truth, and it has been used by writers on Spinoza to support the claim that he held a correspondence theory. There are a number of objections to a correspondence theory in Spinoza.

The statement we have quoted is called an axiom, not a definition, and it might be, therefore, that Spinoza is giving not a definition but a statement of the rationalist belief that ideas—or pure thought—can provide a reliable guide to Nature. A true idea does agree with that of which it is the idea, but this agreement is accidental, in the sense, at least, that it does not serve to *define* what is meant by a true idea. For the truth of an idea is recognized by some intrinsic characteristic, not by the agreement in question.[6]

Spinoza *was* a rationalist, but the denial that he had a correspondence theory of truth, if it is based only on the designation of Axiom 6 as an axiom and not as a definition, is not

---

[6] This is the view of McKeon: "Metaphysically, Spinoza takes it to be certain that a true idea will agree with its object, but the sign of its truth is not such an agreement" (*The Philosophy of Spinoza,* pp. 221–22). I agree that adequacy provides the means by which we can recognize true ideas, but I do not think that "adequate" and "true" are synonyms (see below, pp. 64 f).

especially persuasive. In the first place, the deductive model was an ideal of explanation for Spinoza, not something that he attained with complete success. He did not distinguish rigorously between definitions and axioms.[7] Thus, the designation of the statement under discussion as an axiom may not be significant. Furthermore, there are demonstrations in the *Ethics* whose validity depends on taking Axiom 6 as giving a necessary and sufficient condition of truth, and not simply as a statement of an accidental property of true ideas (see, in particular, E-II, 32, discussed below).

But there is a more serious kind of objection to a correspondence theory in Spinoza. Some have argued that *any* correspondence theory is impossible in Spinoza's metaphysical system.[8] A monistic metaphysics, it is claimed, requires a version of the coherence theory of truth. It is hard to evaluate this argument unless we can make quite clear what is covered by "correspondence theory" and "coherence theory." If correspondence designates a relation that can occur only between two different substances, then, clearly, someone who denies the plurality of substance could not consistently maintain a correspondence view. But if the correspondence theory does not require that the terms of the correspondence relation be different substances, then there is no obvious reason why a monistic metaphysic could not include a correspondence view. Correspondence might refer to a relation between different ways of expressing the single reality—in Spinoza's system, between modes of Thought and modes of Extension. It would be necessary to explain carefully what was meant by

[7] Wolfson goes so far as to say that ". . . the terms 'definitions,' 'axioms,' 'propositions,' and their like are used by Spinoza more or less indiscriminately as conventional labels to be pasted on here and there in order to give to his work the external appearance of a work of geometry" (*The Philosophy of Spinoza*, I, 58).

[8] ". . . a qualified form of the coherence theory of truth is a logically necessary part of Spinoza's system, and of any metaphysical monism or One-Substance doctrine" (Hampshire, *Spinoza*, p. 77).

"Agreement" between an idea and its object, and to show that this agreement could be the basis of a satisfactory definition. If this is possible, a monistic metaphysic would not necessarily rule out all forms of the correspondence theory. Axiom 6 alone is evidence that Spinoza thought it intelligible in his system to talk of the agreement of an idea and its ideatum, but it is not conclusive evidence that he took such agreement to provide a definition of truth. For there are passages where he talks of truth in other ways—for example, his claim that truth is its own criterion—and someone defending a correspondence theory in Spinoza would have to show that these passages are compatible with a correspondence view of truth.

The doctrine that the truth of an idea is to be discovered by examining the inherent characteristics of the idea has also been offered as an objection to a correspondence theory in Spinoza. ". . . puisqu'elle [la vérité] réside dans l'esprit et ne dépend que de lui, il faut qu'au sein de l'esprit elle soit déjà par elle-même quelque chose. La vérité de l'idée vraie ne résulte pas d'une relation de convenance entre cette idée et son objet. . . ." [9] This objection depends in part on the supposition that the object of an idea—its ideatum—must be a mode of Extension. But that is not always the case, as I have pointed out earlier. If the idea and its ideatum were both accessible to thought—were both modes of Thought—then perhaps a sense could be given to "agreement" of idea and ideatum as a definition of truth. We shall develop this in detail further on, but it should be clear already that whatever correspondence theory we work out will differ in important respects from present-day correspondence theories.

Spinoza's various ways of talking about truth have led to confusion. Different commentators have taken one or the other statement to be fundamental, and have claimed on that basis that Spinoza had a coherence view or a correspondence

---

[9] Léon Brunschvicg, *Spinoza et ses contemporains*, p. 21.

view—but either alternative means passing over some of Spinoza's statements. Nor is it enough simply to say that correspondence and coherence definitions are both present.[10] The two theories are believed by many people to be incompatible; if we wish to attribute them both to Spinoza we must show how they are related within his system. We cannot just quote Axiom 6 in support of correspondence and, say, the definition of adequate ideas in support of coherence, and let it go at that.

The preceding discussion has been intended to indicate some of the difficulties in applying either correspondence or coherence unequivocally to Spinoza's theory of truth. Part of the difficulty—as with many other concepts in Spinoza's philosophy—comes about because we approach Spinoza with preconceptions and interpretations that would not have made sense to him, and they lead, as we might expect, to confusion when we apply them to his philosophy. It seems appropriate at this point to undertake a fresh exposition of Spinoza's theory of truth, without concerning ourselves very much at first about which modern theory it most resembles.

e. The definition of truth

In the discussion of substance (Chapter II, above), we saw how Spinoza can adopt a traditional definition, and, by drawing consequences from it and adapting it to his needs, reach a position very different from that of earlier philosophers. He does the same sort of thing, it seems to me, in his theory of truth. The traditional definition of truth was correspondence.[11] In Axiom 6 Spinoza gives us something very like the

[10] *À la* Wolfson. Speaking of correspondence and of what he calls an "internal criterion," Wolfson says that "These two theories of truth are reproduced by Spinoza separately and independently of each other in several places in his work" (*The Philosophy of Spinoza*, II, 99).

[11] The definition goes back to Aristotle: "To say of what is that it is not, or of what is not that it is, is false, while to say of what is that it is, and of what is not that it is not, is true" (*Metaphysics* IV, 6,

traditional definition. Although he calls this an axiom, not a definition, he treats it in his demonstrations as a necessary and sufficient condition of truth. I shall try to show that, as with his conception of substance, Spinoza accepts the traditional formula, but it takes on an altogether new significance in the context of his philosophy.

Taking Axiom 6, then, to give the meaning of "truth," we must explain what it means for an idea to agree with its ideatum. "Idea" and "ideatum" can refer, respectively, to modes of Thought and modes of Extension. An idea, or mode of Thought, is the correlate of some physical object, or mode of Extension. Thus, to say that a true idea agrees with its ideatum is to say that the idea agrees with its correlate in the attribute of Extension. But of course *every* idea agrees with its ideatum in this sense, since Thought and Extension are simply different aspects of a single substance. Every idea has an ideatum, since Thought and Extension are both complete attributes of God, and a mode of Thought cannot but agree with the expression, under the attribute of Extension, of its own content. Therefore every idea must be true, if Axiom 6 is taken as a definition.

This should not come as a surprise to us. Some writers have seen this result as a *reductio ad absurdum* of Spinoza's position,[12] or as a reason not to attribute the correspondence definition to him. But, absurd or not, he is himself the first to point it out:

1011b27). Wolfson says that "The standard theory of truth in the Middle Ages is that of correspondence", and he quotes versions of the theory taken from medieval Jewish and scholastic philosophers (*The Philosophy of Spinoza*, II, 98). That correspondence was the standard medieval theory of truth may be a fair generalization, but, as I shall have occasion to point out, it was not the *only* medieval theory.

[12] Parkinson discusses this point, and concludes: "This means, therefore, that every idea is true, which is absurd; for if the word 'true' is to have its usual sense, there must also be a use for its opposite, 'false' " (*Spinoza's Theory of Knowledge*, p. 113). Parkinson offers no support for the assumption that the word "true" is to have its "usual sense" in Spinoza.

§ All ideas, in so far as they are related to God, are true. (E-II, 32)

> *Omnes ideae, quatenus ad Deum referuntur, verae sunt.*

This is proved as follows:

§ All ideas which are in God always agree with those things of which they are the ideas (Corol. Prop. 7, pt. 2), and therefore (Ax. 6, pt. I) they are all true.

> *Omnes enim ideae, quae in Deo sunt, cum suis ideatis omnino conveniunt (per Coroll. Prop. 7. hujus), adeoque (per Ax. 6. p. 1.) omnes verae sunt.*

The conception of truth here is that of correspondence, and Axiom 6 is used in the demonstration as if it were a definition of truth. (Taken by itself, Axiom 6 might be construed as stating a necessary, but not a sufficient, condition of truth. For from "all true ideas agree with their ideata" it does not follow that all ideas that agree with their ideata are true. But Spinoza's use of the axiom in this demonstration shows that he took the axiom to give a sufficient condition as well. Otherwise the demonstration is fallacious.) [13]

But what of false ideas? If all ideas are true, in the sense we have been discussing, and if "false" is the contradictory of "true," then there can be no false ideas. This is not a very tempting conclusion. But there are a number of ways around it. One could say that although there *is* a sense in which all ideas are true, it does not follow that all ideas are true absolutely. All ideas are true, as Spinoza says, to the extent that they reflect (correspond to) reality (God or Nature being the

---

[13] Joachim's view of Proposition 32 is very different from the one I have suggested. He writes: "Every 'idea' *qua* sustained in that coherent context, is necessarily adequate; or as Spinoza expresses it, 'all ideas as referred to God are true'" (*The Nature of Truth*, p. 153). Joachim, of course, is presenting Spinoza as a coherence theorist. Still, it does seem fair to ask him what he makes of the use of Axiom 6 in the demonstration of this proposition.

complete reality), but not all—in fact hardly any—ideas correspond to reality in every respect. Thus, falsity might not indicate lack of any correspondence *whatever*, for, as part of reality, no idea could fail to express the part of reality that it is. But no idea, except the idea of God, corresponds to reality in *every* respect, so every idea, except the idea of God, must fail to correspond to reality in *some* respect. To claim for an idea the particular correspondence that it lacks is to make a mistake, or to have a false idea. Falsity is the result of trying to make an idea include more than it does. Falsity can only occur for finite minds; it has no place in reality as conceived by the infinite intellect—which is as much as to say that since the infinite idea corresponds to reality in every respect, it is impossible to claim more correspondence for it than it has. Spinoza does talk, sometimes, as if falsity consisted in this kind of stretching of an idea beyond its proper compass:

§ Thus falsity consists only in this, that something is affirmed of a thing, which is not contained in the conception we have formed of that thing, as motion and rest of a semicircle. (*TdIE*, p. 25)

Quare falsitas in hoc solo consistit, quod aliquid de aliqua re affirmetur, quod in ipsius, quam formavimus, conceptu, non continetur, ut motus, vel quies de semicirculo. (*II, 27*)

The conclusion that every idea is true still stands, for every idea does agree with its ideatum. Falsity occurs when an idea is correlated with something not its ideatum.

This way around the difficulty has a number of undesirable features. In particular, it means that "true" and "false" are not contradictory. All ideas are true, since all agree with their ideata, but any idea can be false if it is correlated with things other than its ideatum. Thus, it would make sense to say of a particular idea that it was both true and false (admittedly, however, in different senses). Furthermore, according to the suggested interpretation, truth and falsity no longer depend on inherent properties of the ideas. This may not seem serious to us—many people today would hold that a large class of sentences, if not all, depend for their truth or falsity on the context where they occur. But Spinoza has told us that truth is revealed by the qualities of the idea itself, not its relations with other ideas (quoted above, p. 46).

Another way around the conclusion that all ideas are true would be, having first accepted the conclusion, to go on to develop a different sense of "true," such that "true" *is* the contradictory of "false." Spinoza seems to do this in propositions 33 through 35 of Part II. In Proposition 32, as we have seen, he says that "all ideas, in so far as they are referred to God, are true." In Proposition 33, he says:

§ In ideas there is nothing positive on account of which they are called false.

Nihil in ideis positivum est, propter quod falsae dicuntur.

This proposition arises naturally from the preceding proposition. If all ideas are true, then what do we mean when we say that there are false ideas? Spinoza is saying here that "false" cannot be the contradictory of "true," taking "true" in the sense of Proposition 32. For *every* idea is what it is; it is in God and it expresses *some* reality. That is what was meant in Proposition 32 by saying that all ideas are true. Clearly it is contradictory to suppose that there could be some feature of an idea such that it would not be true in the sense of Proposition 32, for there can be no genuine property of an idea such that an idea does *not* have the reality that it has. To say that there could be is to say that the idea could be and not be in the same respect at the same time. This is the force of Proposition 33.

Having established that there is a general sense of "true," in which it is coextensive with "being," or some other very general term, and that there is no sense of "false" that is opposed to this sense of true—just as there is no sense of "nonbeing" that is opposed to the most general sense of "being"—Spinoza must go on to explain the more common usage in which "true" is the contradictory of "false," and in which it makes sense to speak of a false idea. This is taken up in Proposition 34:

§ Every idea which in us is absolute, or adequate and perfect, is true.

Omnis idea, quae in nobis est absoluta, sive adaequata, & perfecta, vera est.

Here the adequacy or perfection of an idea *in us* provides a sense of "true" in which it makes sense to say that some ideas are true and others false. An idea that is adequate in us is true, in this new sense, and one that is not adequate in us is false. All ideas are adequate in God, and so, for God, all ideas are true—which is another way of stating Proposition 32.

Our interpretation so far has gone as follows: Spinoza accepts the correspondence definition of truth, but it leads him to the conclusion that every idea is true, since in his system every idea corresponds to *some* reality. "True" thus becomes a very general term, analogous to "existent" or "real." If it is to make sense to talk of true *and* of false ideas, we need another sense of "true" which will permit a distinction between "true" and "false." This new sense is offered in Proposition 34. In the new sense, "true" means "adequate" or "perfect," and "false," presumably, means "inadequate" or "imperfect." We resolve the question of correspondence and coherence by saying that both are present, on different levels, and with different functions in Spinoza's philosophy.

One difficulty with this interpretation is that Spinoza does not *say* he is using more than one sense of "true." But perhaps we could reply to that by saying that no one can be expected to develop explicitly all the consequences of everything he says. If we are interested in working out those consequences, and not just in summarizing Spinoza's words, we should perhaps expect to encounter doctrines or points of view that Spinoza does not formulate himself, but which appear to be required by what he does say.

There is, however, a more serious difficulty. We have seen that the demonstration of Proposition 32 uses a correspondence view of truth; Axiom 6, Part I, is there given the status of a definition. Proposition 34, which we have described as introducing a different sense of "true," is demonstrated as follows:

§ When we say that an adequate and perfect idea is given in us, we say nothing else than (Corol. Prop. 11, Part II) that an adequate and perfect idea exists in God in so far as He constitutes the essence of our mind, and consequently (Prop. 32, Part II) we say nothing else than that this idea is true.

Cum dicimus, dari in nobis ideam adaequatam, & perfectam, nihil aliud dicimus (per Coroll. Prop. 11. hujus), quam quod in Deo, quatenus nostrae Mentis essentiam constituit, detur idea adaequata, & perfecta, & consequenter (per Prop. 32. hujus), nihil aliud dicimus, quam quod talis idea sit vera.

We see that the demonstration of Proposition 34 relies on Proposition 32. Consequently if there *is* a new sense of "true" in Proposition 34, the demonstration is not acceptable, for it involves an equivocation on the sense of "true." Proposition 32 takes the definition from Axiom 6; an idea is true if and only if it agrees with that of which it is the idea. But Proposition 34 appears to take adequacy and perfection as defining features of truth. We cannot prove anything about truth in sense number 2 on the basis of a proposition about truth in sense number 1. If we wish to avoid equivocation, we must use only one sense—but which one? Both formulations appear frequently in Spinoza's writing, and neither can be swept under the rug without doing violence to many passages. But if we accept them both, Spinoza is found to have committed an elementary logical error. Furthermore, if we accept them both we have the problem of explaining their relations to one another more fully, and of explaining why Spinoza never talks as if "true" were ambiguous.

We confront here the basic problem of truth in Spinoza, which takes its clearest form in propositions 32–40, especially 32 and 34. Here the two theories of truth are stated clearly, but the cross references between different propositions require that there be no difference between the two theories of truth, if the demonstrations are to be logically acceptable. By taking one definition over the other, commentators have attributed different theories of truth to Spinoza without ever facing the difficulty we have raised, and by saying that both theories are present the difficulty is indicated, but not solved. The problem of interpretation can be worked out, I believe, if we recall certain features of the idea/ideatum distinction, and of the conception of substance. I shall digress, therefore, to call attention to the relevant points.

In discussing the agreement of idea and ideatum, we have been treating ideas as modes of Thought and ideata as modes of Extension. But we saw earlier that this is a simplification. The distinction between idea and ideatum does not always coincide with the distinction between Thought and Extension. Thus, saying that a true idea must agree with its ideatum does not mean only that a mode of Thought, to be true, must agree with its correlate mode of Extension. Some ideas have other ideas, not modes of Extension, as their ideata. "Ideatum" is simply a word for that part of reality presented by an idea. An idea, as a mode of Thought—that is, as part of the system of ideas included in the attribute of Thought— can be the object or ideatum of another idea, and the new idea gives a different expression of the reality expressed by its ideatum. In Spinoza's terminology, an idea as it is in its relation to the rest of reality—as it is in itself—has *essentia formalis*. When the idea is considered as having an ideatum, then it has an *essentia objectiva*.

In its *essentia objectiva*, a true idea is simply a particular expression of reality; it is reality thought about. But we must remember that neither the idea/ideatum distinction nor the *essentia objectiva/essentia formalis* distinction coincides with the distinction between Thought and Extension. Idea and ideatum *may* be modes, respectively, of Thought and Extension, but they do not have to be. They may both be modes of Thought.[14]

The *essentia objectiva* of the idea agrees with the *essentia formalis* of its ideatum. They are, after all, the same thing. Which is like saying that an idea agrees with that of which it is the idea, or that the idea is true. Truth—the truth of something—is its idea, or its *essentia objectiva*. Spinoza says, "The true idea of Peter is the reality of Peter represented objectively" (*TdIE*, p. 12). This is clearer still in Latin: "vera autem idea Petri est essentia Petri objectiva" (II, 14). Thus, truth is *essentia objectiva; being* as represented by the intellect; reality expressed under the attribute of Thought. As Spinoza says:

§ Certainty is nothing else than the objective essence of a thing. (*TdIE*, p. 12)

Hinc patet, quod certitudo nihil sit praeter ipsam essentiam objectivam; . . . (II, 15)

The least confusing way of describing the idea/ideatum distinction is in terms of *essentia objectiva* and *essentia formalis*. But however the distinction is explained, the important point

---

[14] Joachim's inability to explain Spinoza's concept of method—reflexive knowledge—comes about because he supposes that the ideatum of an idea must be a mode of Extension (*Spinoza's Tractatus*, p. 105). Louis Terrasse makes the same supposition ("La Doctrine Spinoziste de la vérité, p. 216).

is that idea and ideatum are, in the end, different aspects of a single reality. There is no metaphysical separation between them. Since they are not metaphysically separate, an idea inevitably agrees with its ideatum; it *is* its ideatum. This agreement is not always evident to us, with our finite minds. We can return now to the argument broken off on p. 61, and to the resolution of the apparently different definitions of truth.

In Proposition 32, Spinoza says that all ideas are true "in so far as they are referred to God." In the demonstration, and in the demonstration of Proposition 33, he again talks of ideas that are "in God." Now, the proof of Proposition 32 includes a reference to Proposition 7, corollary, in which we are told that God's power of thought is equal to his power of action. That is to say, every mode of Thought has a corresponding mode of Extension, or, better, every idea in God is present also as ideatum. There are no ideas without ideata, and no ideata without ideas. For the truth of an idea to be recognized, both idea and ideatum must be grasped; that is, to recognize truth—the agreement of idea and ideatum—is to understand the identity of idea and ideatum. The special feature of ideas "in God"—the reason Spinoza includes the qualification "in so far as they are referred to God" in Proposition 32—is that in God the unity or "agreement" of ideas and their ideata is always evident. Any mode of substance is contained in God *both* as idea and as ideatum, so the truth of the idea is always evident. In God there is no idea that is not understood to be true.

But in a finite intellect it could happen that an idea had no ideatum to correspond. In that case the idea would not be true in the finite intellect—its truth, that is, would not be understood by the finite intellect. This is the basis of Spinoza's distinction between ideas that are adequate and perfect "in us," and those that are adequate and perfect "in God." For truth to be recognized, both sides of the identity (of idea and

ideatum) must be present. This always happens in God, but
only rarely in humans. Modes of Extension, in particular,
cannot be present in immediate and complete fashion to a
human mind, and so our knowledge of particular physical objects is inevitably incomplete. (This last point is further de-
veloped in Chapter IV.)

We can, however, form true ideas of ideas. For in the case
of ideas of ideas, idea and ideatum can both be present in
our minds. The idea is understood as the idea of *this* ideatum; it contains its *essentia objectiva*. But since the ideatum
(by hypothesis) is also present, we have its *essentia formalis*
in our mind too. To understand the identity of idea and ideatum is to see that the *essentia objectiva* posited by the idea
coincides precisely with the *essentia formalis* of the ideatum.
We understand, for example, that our definition of a triangle
as a three-sided figure is correct, because we recognize at the
same time that a triangle *is* a three-sided figure.

In slightly different terminology, the ideatum is *understood;* that is, we have a true idea of it, which is to *know* it.
When this happens we have an adequate and perfect idea, an
idea whose identity with its ideatum is immediately grasped
by our mind. This is the only kind of true idea we can have;
truth for us always takes the form of reflective knowledge. If
the idea and ideatum *are* equally present in our mind, then
nothing else is required to know that we have a true idea. If
we understand an idea *as* the idea of a specific ideatum, also
present in our mind—that is, if we apprehend in our mind
the unity of idea and ideatum—then nothing more can be required for us to know that we have a true idea. Understanding a true idea is necessary and sufficient.

It turns out, therefore, that it *is* the agreement—or identity
—of idea and ideatum that serves to define truth, and there is
no second sense of truth involved when Spinoza speaks, in
Proposition 34, of ideas that are "adequate and perfect." "Adequacy" and "perfection" describe characteristics of true

ideas; they do not define truth. Adequacy and perfection are the properties by which we recognize true ideas, but "adequate" and "true" are not synonyms.

Spinoza is careful to distinguish between adequacy and truth in his definitions. "Truth" means agreement with reality; "A true idea must agree with that of which it is the idea." "Adequate" means "self-sufficient," or "self-explanatory":

§ By adequate idea I mean an idea which in so far as it is considered in itself, without reference to the object, has all the properties or internal signs of a true idea. (E-II, Def. 4)

Per ideam adaequatam intelligo ideam, quae, quatenus in se sine relatione ad objectum consideratur, omnes verae ideae proprietates, sive denominationes intrinsecas habet.

Spinoza explains this definition, so as to distinguish adequacy still further from truth:

§ I say internal so as to exclude that which is external, the agreement, namely, of the idea with its object.

Dico intrinsecas, ut illam secludam, quae extrinseca est, nempe convenientiam ideae cum suo ideato.

He makes a similar distinction in Letter 60:

§ I recognize no other difference between a true and an adequate idea than that the word true refers only to the agreement of the idea with its ideatum, while the word adequate refers to the nature of the idea in itself; so that there is really no difference between a true and an adequate idea except this extrinsic relation. (*Correspondence*, p. 300)

Inter ideam veram & adaequatam nullam aliam differentiam agnosco, quam quod nomen veri respiciat tantummodo convenientiam ideae cum suo ideato; Nomen adaequati autem naturam ideae in se ipsa; ita ut revera nulla detur differentia inter ideam veram, & adaequatam praeter relationem illam extrinsecam. (*IV*, 270)

Although truth is defined as agreement of idea and ideatum, we are rather far from the correspondence theory of truth as ordinarily understood. As he so often does, Spinoza retains the conventional terminology while giving it a special significance, intelligible only in the context of the rest of his philosophy.

Spinoza is now in a position to explain falsity. The nature of falsity follows quite easily from the discussion we have just given. If there can be true ideas only when we have idea and ideatum immediately present, and grasp their identity, then whenever we do not grasp an idea as the adequate expression of its ideatum we cannot have a true idea. It is precisely this lack of knowledge that Spinoza calls falsity.

§ Falsity consists in the privation of knowledge, which inadequate, that is to say, mutilated and confused ideas involve. (E-II, 35)

Falsitas consistit in cognitionis privatione, quam ideae inadaequatae, sive mutilatae, & confusae involvunt.

This interpretation does make "false" the contradictory of "true." The *meaning* of "truth" and "falsity" is the same for both finite and infinite minds—although an infinite mind contains no instances of inadequate ideas, because *as* infinite mind it contains all expressions of reality. But since the definitions are the same for men as for God, we can perhaps see why

§ . . . it must be that the clear and distinct ideas of the mind are as true as those of God. (E-II, 43, note)

. . . *adeoque tam necesse est, ut Mentis clarae, & distinctae ideae verae sint, ac Dei ideae.*

When we see the relation, and the distinction between truth and adequacy, we can see why some of Descartes's problems do not arise for Spinoza. For if someone has a clear and distinct idea, it follows from the nature of substance or reality that the idea is true. Spinoza does not need to find an external guarantee for his clear and distinct ideas, or to worry about malign demons or deceiving Gods. Instead, he recognizes that the search for an external guarantee leads to an infinite regress. But although Spinoza's position differs from Descartes's in the ways we have mentioned, there are important similarities too, and both views encounter similar difficulties. Descartes and Spinoza take clear and distinct ideas as their model of true understanding; for both of them the highest form of knowledge is intuitive. But this means that the highest kind of knowledge is a direct personal experience which by its nature is incommunicable. There is an appeal to "mental seeing," and such an appeal makes knowledge into something mysterious or even mystical. Furthermore, what is intuitively obvious to one person may be obscure to another.

The second point—that what is intuitive to one person may not be intuitive to another—does not need to cause Spinoza any difficulty. When he introduces the three kinds of knowledge in E-II, 40, scholium, he gives us the definitions and then he says "All this I will explain by one example" (E-II, 40, note 2). In *TdIE* he also illustrates the different kinds of knowledge with a single example. The use of one example shows that a particular subject matter can be known by one mode of cognition *or* by another; the kinds of knowledge are ways of grasping things, and what is at one time grasped discursively—by the second kind of knowledge—could, at another time or by another person, be grasped by the third kind. Thus, Spinoza tells us that "the things I have been able to know by this kind of knowledge are as yet very few" (*TdIE*, p. 9), and it is clear from this (and from E-V, 28) that what we know discursively at one time we can come to know intuitively.

I am not sure that Spinoza can meet the first objection— the claim that he has made knowing into something private and incommunicable. However, it may be that he does not regard this as a defect in his theory. To the contrary, he appears to recognize and accept it:

§ The third kind of knowledge depends upon the mind as its formal cause. . . . (E-V, 31)

Tertium cognitionis genus pendet a Mente, tanquam a formali causa. . . .

The discovery of truth—salvation, in effect—is for Spinoza intensely personal, and we shall have occasion to point out in Chapter V that there is a sense in which the third kind of knowledge is self-knowledge. The reasons for this will emerge better after we have examined the relation between truth and God or substance, which we shall do in Chapter IV. But it does not follow from what we have been saying that what we know by the third kind of knowledge has no intersubjective validity. The reasons for this, too, will emerge better in the next chapter.

Spinoza's position is remarkable when we recall that it does not involve new verbal expressions, either of "substance" or of "truth." Rather, we are dealing with strict applications of formulae that were part of the philosophical tradition. But despite the verbal agreement of Spinoza's definition with earlier definitions, I hope it is clear by now that it will not do simply to say that he has a correspondence theory of truth. And I hope it is clear that it is equally misleading to say that he has a coherence theory of truth. "Truth," like "substance," receives a special interpretation in Spinoza's system, and, like his theory of substance, Spinoza's theory of truth depends on his metaphysical orientation for its intelligibility.

IV. Truth and substance

a. Knowledge of finite modes

THE UNDERSTANDING of a true idea, that is, the recognition that an idea agrees with its ideatum, depends on an immediate grasp of both idea and ideatum; a grasp, in fact, of their identity. This is an intuitive understanding of the essence of the idea *as* identical with its ideatum. Spinoza calls knowledge of this kind "intuitive science" or "the third kind of knowledge" and he considers it the most desirable kind of knowledge. It is not the only reliable knowledge; reasoning which draws conclusions by argument can give valid results, even though the relation of the ideas is not present in a single apprehension. But argument of this kind depends for its validity on some grasp of true ideas. Even sensuous experience yields information that is reliable for some purposes. But intuitive science is the only form of adequate and perfect knowledge; sensuous experience cannot lead us to genuine understanding.

Physical objects are revealed to us by images, and an image describes only the physical effect of some other body on our body. The idea or image that we have of a physical object does not "agree with that of which it is the idea," except in a very superficial and fragmentary way. The image is determined, among other things, by the object that causes it, so that it reflects the nature of its cause to some extent. But it also reflects the nature of other things, notably the body in which it is produced. The relation of an image to its cause is clearly not the relation of identity that we find when an idea agrees with its ideatum. But it is this latter relation that gives us a true idea. We might, in certain cases, wish to say that our ideas of physical reality correspond to the facts, or that they are true, but we are using "true" very loosely. We could not speak of adequate understanding of physical objects. For that we would need a complete grasp of the causal relations between things, which everyone agrees that we do not have. We cannot attain the comprehension of a mode of Extension that would render it self-explanatory, and so our encounter with it cannot be dignified by the name "knowledge."

We are finite beings, and a finite intellect, by definition, is one that does not include ideas of *all* modes of Extension. But in order to have an adequate understanding of a body, we would need to understand its causal relations with other bodies. That is to say, we would have to have, as our ideatum—the ideatum of the idea that constitutes our mind—not just a single finite body, but also that body together with all other bodies that affect it. There is no limit, short of the physical universe taken as a whole, to the bodies that would have to be included:

§ An individual thing, or a thing which is finite and which has a determinate existence, cannot exist nor be determined to action unless it be determined to existence and action by another cause which is also finite and has a determinate existence; and again, this cause cannot exist nor be determined to action unless by another cause which is also finite and determined to existence and action, and so on *ad infinitum*. (E-I, 28)

Quodcunque singulare, sive quaevis res, quae finita est, & determinatam habet existentiam, non potest existere, nec ad operandum determinari, nisi ad existendum, & operandum determinetur ab alia causa, quae etiam finita est, & determinatam habet existentiam: & rursus haec causa non potest etiam existere, neque ad operandum determinari, nisi ab alia, quae etiam finita est, & determinatam habet existentiam, determinetur ad existendum, & operandum, & sic in infinitum.

Adequate knowledge of *any* mode of Extension entails knowledge of *all* modes of Extension, which in turn requires an infinite intellect.

Since our acquaintance with modes of Extension is not based on understanding, we must rely on "brute" facts, which present themselves without reasons and which we must accept without full explanation. Empirical knowledge can never be certain, since it rests somewhere on a brute fact, and so there is possibility of error. For finite intellects there will always be synthetic statements, whose truth must simply be *accepted* and not grasped by understanding the statement.

Spinoza is frequently described as an advocate of an a priori science, in which all knowledge would be reached by deduction from clear and distinct ideas. This is a misinterpretation, at least if "all knowledge" is supposed to include knowledge of physical reality and if science is supposed to be something attainable by humans. We cannot investigate nature by deduction, even though we try to arrange our knowledge, once acquired, in the most satisfying intellectual order —that is, in a deductive system—which is the best form of explanation. Empirical knowledge remains unexplained some-where, resting as it does on images, whereas Spinoza's ideal of understanding requires that there be no brute or unex-plained facts. Far from advocating a deductive investigation of matters of fact, Spinoza's position is that modes of Exten-sion cannot be known, in a strict sense, at all.[1]

The preceding remarks have been too restricted in one re-spect at least; in discussing modes of Extension we may have given the impression that our inability to know modes of Ex-tension comes about because of some peculiarity of the attri-bute of Extension. This is not the case. There is nothing about modes of Extension *qua* Extension that makes them unknow-able; it is because they are *finite*, and we are finite, that we cannot know individual modes of Extension. Proposition 28, Part I, which we quoted above, does not speak of modes of Extension but of "An individual thing, or a thing which is finite and which has a determinate existence. . . ." There is no restriction of this proposition to a particular attribute. Thus, what we have said in the last few pages about modes of Extension applies equally to finite modes of Thought. *Any* finite mode is unknowable by a finite intellect.

The possibility of a finite mind's having true ideas does not violate this principle. For true ideas are not finite modes of Thought. They are, as we have seen, "Equally in the part and in the whole." This means (1) that true ideas are infinite. They are not determined by any particular mode of sub-stance; instead they follow from the nature of substance itself (see, in this connection, the demonstration of E-I, 28); and (2) that true ideas are a priori, in the sense of being unfalsifi-able by experience, since if they are not determined by any individual mode of substance, then, a fortiori, they cannot be

---

[1] Spinoza's view of empirical knowledge and experimental science, and his conviction that they can never provide adequate rational under-standing, are well discussed by McKeon, *The Philosophy of Spinoza*, Part I, Chapter IV, "Spinoza and Experimental Science."

falsified by an individual mode of substance. Spinoza does not express himself in the terminology that I have just been using, but I think that the conclusion we have reached does follow from E-I, 28, and its demonstration.

We might agree that statements that cannot be falsified are a priori statements and that the only unfalsifiable knowledge is a priori knowledge. We might even accept some of Spinoza's examples of certain (unfalsifiable) knowledge. But we would perhaps deny that what we are dealing with here is a manifestation of the essence of reality. We would be more likely to speak of "conventions" that underlie our a priori beliefs, and we might not think it self-contradictory for two people to have different sets of a priori beliefs. Some people, indeed, would go so far as to say that *any* statement can be regarded as true a priori if we are prepared to make appropriate adjustments elsewhere in our beliefs about the world. But for Spinoza, a priori knowledge was not a matter of belief or convention. He thought that some ideas were true, and could be known to be true, and that they provided an understanding of reality itself.

b. Truth and substance

That true ideas provide an understanding of "reality itself" for Spinoza can, I think, be taken quite literally. As I have pointed out, we cannot have true or adequate ideas of physical objects, for to do so we would have to possess in ourselves the whole physical universe. But Spinoza says that we can have *some* true ideas. For an idea to be true in us, its idea and ideatum must be present to us in the same way they are present to God, and conversely, something that *was* present to us as to God could only be true, since all ideas in God are true. Or, in Spinoza's terms, things that are "common to everything, and which are equally in the part and in the whole, can only be adequately conceived" (E-II, 38. Latin text, see p. 49). Something present "equally in the part and in the whole" would be present to us in the same way that it was present to God. Which is to say that an idea of this kind would be adequate in us—or in any other finite mind.

We have given examples earlier of how laws of logic, or axioms of geometry, can be used to illustrate this point, and there is no need to repeat the earlier discussion. We have also discussed how, for Spinoza, knowing any finite mode of God means knowing its cause, and the causal chain can be traced back, ultimately, to God. Perfect understanding would have to be self-contained; it could not be logically dependent on something that was not part of the explanation. We do not actually have an understanding of the physical universe, but if we consider what it would be like fully to understand something, we are led to conceive, as the ideal that we would like to attain, a logically independent explanation—one that could be understood in itself. "Every idea of any body or actually existing individual thing necessarily involves the eternal and infinite essence of God" (E-II, 45. Latin text, see p. 49).

What all this means is that to understand something is to understand God, since "understanding" something means, strictly, having an explanation that can be understood "in itself," and "being understood in itself" is precisely the definition of God or substance. The adequate and self-sufficient nature of God is something "present equally in the part and in the whole." In grasping a true idea we grasp something that is complete in itself—that is, we grasp the nature of God or substance.

This seems to me an important conclusion, for it leads to an identification of truth and substance. We can work out the identification in various ways. Truth, as we have seen, is its own criterion, which means that a true idea is known to be true once it is understood, and it requires no explanation outside itself. Clearly, we could say on this basis that a true idea is "That which is in itself and is conceived through itself; in other words, that the conception of which does not need the conception of another thing from which it must be formed" (E-I, def. 3. Latin text, see p. 8). A true idea satisfies the requirements of this definition. But it is the definition of Substance, not of truth. In saying that truth is its own criterion, Spinoza may be interpreted as saying that it is one form of substance—or better, one of the infinitely many ways of conceiving substance. To have a true idea is to conceive the essence of God or substance.

Still another way of saying this is to say that truth is an expression of *causa sui*. Spinoza defines *causa sui* as

§ . . . that whose essence involves existence, or that whose nature cannot be understood unless existing. (E-I, def. 1)

Per causam sui intelligo id, cujus essentia involvit existentiam, sive id, cujus natura non potest concipi, nisi existens.

He is talking here of being, a more general category than truth, since although truth or ideas describe one form that being can take, being can take other forms as well, such as Extension. But we can see truth as a special form of *causa sui* by substituting a particular kind of being for the general category "existence" in the definition of *causa sui*. Thus, truth is "that whose essence involves adequacy, or that whose nature cannot be understood unless true or adequate." This is very close to the view of truth as its own criterion.

Spinoza does not equate truth and substance as explicitly as I have done. But it seems to me that the identification of truth and substance does follow from what he says, and I shall try to develop it further, even though this will sometimes mean relying on argument rather than on Spinoza's actual words. Much that he does say becomes clearer, I think, if we develop the parallel between truth and substance, and there are places where he comes very close to stating it himself. Some of the passages already quoted in connection with truth as its own criterion can be used to support the relation

—metaphysically the identity—between truth and substance; and in addition there are passages such as this one from *TdIE:*

§ . . . thought is said to be true, if it involves objectively the essence of any principle which has no cause, and is known through and in itself. (*TdIE*, p. 24)

Cogitatio enim vera etiam dicitur, quae essentiam alicujus principii objective involvit, quod causam non habet, & per se, & in se cognoscitur. (*II, 26*)

or this from the Ethics:

§ . . . with regard to the difference between a true and a false idea, it is evident from Prop. 35 Pt. II that the former is related to the latter as being is to nonbeing. (E-II, 43, note)

Nam quod ad differentiam inter ideam veram, & falsam attinet, constat ex Propositione 35. hujus, illam ad hanc sese habere, ut ens ad non-ens.

Note also several places where Spinoza uses the expression

§ truly . . . that is to say (Ax. 6, pt. I), as they are in themselves. (E-II, 44, dem. See also the demonstration of the corollary.)

. . . vere percipere, nempe (per Ax. 6. p. 1.) ut in se sunt. . . .

The union of truth and substance gives content to Spinoza's claim that we can have an adequate knowledge of God.

§ The human mind possesses an adequate knowledge of the eternal and infinite essence of God. (E-II, 47)

Mens humana adaequatam habet cognitionem aeternae, & infinitae essentiae Dei.

In this claim Spinoza contradicts the medieval tradition, which denied that we could know the essence of God. Spinoza's view, partly, perhaps, because it *does* go against estab-

lished ways of thinking, has been trivialized or even contradicted.[2] Some writers have said that all he means to point out
is that, since everything that is is in God, we cannot know
anything that is not a part of God or substance. This interpretation does give one of Spinoza's doctrines, but it is not what
he means when he says that we can have an adequate idea of
the essence of God. Nor does his claim represent a confusion
on his part between finite and infinite ideas; it is not necessary, in saying that man can know the essence of God, to
deny man's status as a finite mode. To say that we have an
adequate idea of God is another way of saying that we have
an adequate idea. For any idea that is adequate in Spinoza's
sense of being self-explanatory and true by virtue of being
understood is a manifestation of *causa sui,* that is, of God's essence. For God's essence is precisely the property of being,
and being understood, "in itself." Thus, to have an adequate
idea is to understand the essence of substance, as given in the
definition. An adequate idea presents an infinite being, "infinite" in that it is complete in itself and cannot be limited by
anything.

Someone could object that a true idea is not really substance, or the essence of substance; it is only an *instance,* one
example out of many, since there are many true ideas and
only one substance. But this objection does not hold up. We
have more than one true idea, but we have independent

---

[2] Wolfson, for instance, tells us that ". . . Spinoza's substance is in-
conceivable, and its essence undefinable and hence unknowable" (*The
Philosophy of Spinoza* I, 76). This is indefensible as an exposition of
Spinoza's views. One could claim not to understand what Spinoza
means when he says that he has a clear understanding of God (although
I shall try to suggest an explanation), but that this was Spinoza's position is not debatable. "To your question whether I have as clear an idea
of God as I have of a triangle, I answer in the affirmative" (Letter LVI,
Correspondence, p. 289). The reasons for Wolfson's misinterpretation
are convincingly set forth by E. M. Curley, *Spinoza's Metaphysics,* pp.
28–36.

grounds for denying the plurality of substance. The essence of substance is unique, and it is this unique essence that is discovered in any idea that we recognize to be true. From which it follows that our true ideas are different expressions of the one substance. The possession of more than one true idea is not evidence either that there is more than one substance, or that ideas do not actually reveal the essence of substance. For substance can be expressed in an infinitude of ways—there are infinitely many manifestations of the single essence of substance.

In another sense, however, we *could* say that an adequate idea is not a complete manifestation of God, for it expresses God's essence in only one of the infinite ways in which God's essence can be expressed. A true idea is God's essence expressed under the attribute of Thought: it *is* God's essence, and hence infinite, but Thought is only one of God's attributes, and so the adequate idea does not exhaust God's being. It is a genuine expression of *causa sui,* but it is not the *only* way of expressing *causa sui.* Spinoza expresses this doctrine by talking of "infinite modes in infinite ways." Joachim offers the following formulation: "God, we may say, is revealed whole in each Attribute, but *differently* in each, and *wholly* only in all of them together." [3]

If to have a true idea is to understand God, we can explain the superficial confusion in *TdIE* where Spinoza says sometimes that method consists in understanding a true idea and at other times that it consists in having the idea of God. We see now that there is no difference: to have a true idea *is* to understand the essence of God. Thus, Spinoza's demonstrations that we do have true ideas are equally demonstrations that we know the essence of God, traditional theology notwithstanding.

The close relation between truth and adequacy comes

[3] *The Nature of Truth,* p. 150.

about because the two concepts are consequences of Spinoza's conception of reality or of substance. An idea that corresponds to reality—a true idea—must express the essence of *causa sui* or substance, and thus the idea will be self-explanatory—understood through itself. One might object that it would be possible for an idea to *express* reality without *sharing* its defining features. But Spinoza's doctrine that the idea *is* its ideatum rules out that possibility: the objection would make a metaphysical separation between ideas and their objects, so that although the *essentia objectiva* contained in an idea might express self-sufficient being, that would not be sufficient to establish that the *essentia formalis* of the ideatum is also an expression of self-sufficient being. This would undermine the one-substance doctrine. Spinoza's monism *does* rule out those forms of the correspondence theory that require metaphysically different—independent— kinds of things to serve as terms in the correspondence relations.

We can see now, also, why Spinoza says that the order of the intellect is one and the same for everyone. The order of the intellect is the order of ideas; when we have a true idea, we understand the essence of reality. Reality is single, and *any* understanding is thus a revelation of the *one* reality. Since there is only one God or substance, and since having an adequate idea involves understanding God or substance, it would be contradictory to talk of two people who had an adequate idea of something and yet disagreed. The unity of reality, which provides the basis for certainty, and guarantees for everyone the validity of true ideas, can also be described in terms of "common notions." Common notions, or axioms, form the foundations of our reasoning, and we can understand now why they are valid for all.

The connection between truth and substance has not been made explicit in the secondary literature on Spinoza. The only full-length treatment of Spinoza's theory of truth, to my knowledge, is by Raphaël Lévêque, *Le Problème de la vérité dans la philophie de Spinoza* (Strasbourg, 1923). Lévêque's great shortcoming, in my opinion, is that despite his title he does not take time to discuss explicitly Spinoza's definition of truth, or to discuss alternative definitions. Nor is there any attempt to relate the concepts of truth and substance as defined by Spinoza.

Lévêque does speak in one passage of substance as "vérité première," by which he seems to mean that substance is a sort of axiom which provides the ultimate link between Thought and Extension, thus assuring that ideas are true (in the sense of corresponding to their objects) and this comes about because substance is simultaneously essence *and* existence:

> Il faut que le point de départ du système soit l'essence enveloppant l'existence. . . . Si donc on veut que le système du vrai ne soit pas une pure phénoménologie, mais corresponde à une réalité, il est nécessaire qu'à l'origine de ce système on se place d'emblée au sein du réel ou de l'être; par là, on établira que les choses sont dans la réalité ou formellement ce qu'elles sont dans la représentation ou objectivement" (p. 55).

Further on, however, Lévêque speaks of truth in typical coherence fashion: "Ce qui est réel et, par suite, ce qui est vrai, c'est donc uniquement l'Univers lui-même, la Totalité" (p. 107), and later still he identifies "truth" with "reality." But "reality" is understood here as opposed to "appearance" or "illusion," so that the distinction between understanding and imagination becomes a distinction between what is genuine and what is illusory. This account makes an idealist of Spinoza, and Lévêque follows through with other idealist positions; that God is unknowable: ". . . étant lui-même ineffable il ne peut nous être révélé sans être, par là, transformé" (p. 136), and that the attribute of Thought is the "most fundamental" of the attributes (pp. 134 ff). Thus, when Lévêque connects "truth" with "reality" it is not at all clear what is intended, "truth" being undefined and "reality" having become largely an honorific term. We shall have more to say about the "idealization" of Spinoza in the next section.

In relating the concept of truth to the concept of substance it has not been my intention to present Spinoza as an idealist, or as a materialist (either alternative seems to me wrong), but to point out the logical similarity of the two concepts. The same sort of logical structure is found in the concept of freedom, which I take up in Chapter V. First, however, we can sum up and conclude our discussion of the coherence theory of truth.

c. Coherence theory: conclusion

In the light of our identification of truth with substance, we may summarize Spinoza's divergence from the usual form of the coherence theory of truth. We have, I think, shown in Chapter III that Spinoza does not accept the usual form of the coherence definition of truth, nor does he accept coherence as the criterion of truth, if by "coherence criterion" we mean the claim that the truth of an idea is ascertained by examining its relations to other ideas. A further claim of coherence theorists is that since the only perfectly true idea is the idea of the whole, we can have no perfectly true ideas. Instead our ideas—or judgments—are "more or less" true. Spinoza agrees that the idea of the whole, or of God, is the only idea that is perfectly true. But for him it does not follow from this that we have no true ideas, but that all our true ideas must be manifestations of the idea of God or substance. There can be indefinitely many manifestations of the essence of substance, and all of them are true. Conversely, any true idea is, *ipso facto,* a manifestation of the essence of substance. From this we are, I think, justified in concluding that Spinoza would reject the doctrine of degrees of truth commonly associated with the coherence theory. Spinoza *does* agree that we can have no adequate ideas of finite modes, so that as regards empirical knowledge one might make out a case for a doctrine of degrees of truth, but this interpretation would apply only to the first kind of knowledge and the *definition* of truth would remain the agreement of idea and ideatum. (It is *because* truth means agreement of idea and ideatum that we cannot have true ideas of modes of Extension.)

For Spinoza one reason we cannot have adequate knowledge of finite modes is that each finite mode is related to every other. The claim that each individual thing is related to every other individual thing is frequently associated with the view that all of a thing's relations with other things are essential to the thing's being what it is. These are different theories, and neither one implies the other. Nevertheless, they are not always kept separate, and they are often lumped together as part of the theory of internal relations. A third position is sometimes included too: the view that the being of an individual thing consists *only* in its relations with other things. Spinoza does believe that the universe is coherently ordered, and that every finite mode is causally related to every other. Furthermore, he does not distinguish logical from causal relations. It is reasonable, therefore, to attribute to him some form of the doctrine of internal relations. But the precise form of the doctrine of internal relations that we ought to ascribe to Spinoza is a difficult question. I shall not try to work it out in detail, but I will at least indicate one form that it does *not* take in Spinoza. Joachim attributes to Spinoza a theory of internal relations similar to his own (and that of other English idealists) [4] and this is certainly wrong. Spinoza indisputably holds that an individual thing has causal relations with other

---

[4] A finite thing ". . . owes its *existence* to an indefinite chain of causes, each of which is itself a finite body and the effect of another finite body: it owes its *nature* to its place in the whole system of bodies which together constitute the corporeal universe. . . . 'it' is through and through constituted by its relations . . ." *A Study of the Ethics of Spinoza*, p. 23.

things, and since to know something is to know its cause we could not have knowledge of an individual thing without going beyond the thing itself, and examining its relations with other things. But this is not to say (as Joachim would have us do) that the essence of an individual thing *consists* in its relations with other things. Spinoza tells us that

§ . . . the essences of particular mutable things are not to be gathered from their series or order of existence, which would furnish us with nothing beyond their extrinsic denominations, their relations, or, at most, their circumstances, all of which are very different from their inmost essence. This inmost essence must be sought solely from fixed and eternal things. (*TdIE*, p. 34)

. . . *rerum singularium mutabilium essentiae non sunt depromendae ab earum serie, sive ordine existendi; cum hic nihil aliud nobis praebeat praeter denominationes extrinsecas, relationes, aut ad summum circumstantias: quae omnia longe absunt ab intima essentia rerum. Haec vero tantum est petenda a fixis, atque aeternis rebus.* . . . (*II*, 36–37) [5]

Thus, we see that of the three doctrines mentioned at the beginning of the previous paragraph, Spinoza accepts the first but not the second or third. For this reason I say that Spinoza holds a "form" of the theory of internal relations, which is sufficient for our present purpose, namely to settle the question of the coherence theory of truth. Whatever the details of Spinoza's view of the essences of individual things, he did believe that nature was arranged in a coherent, intelligible, fashion.

But a coherence theory of nature is not the same thing as a coherence theory of truth. It is perhaps a necessary condition for a coherence theory of truth, and if so a person supporting coherence as a view of truth would also support a coherence

---

[5] Some discussion of the essences of individual things is found in Curley, *Spinoza's Metaphysics*, pp. 22–24.

view of nature. But the belief that the universe is a coherent whole is not a sufficient condition for a coherence definition of truth; it does not *entail* a definition of truth as coherence, nor does it entail that no proposition can be wholly true.[6]

From the preceding discussion, we see that, although Spinoza does not define truth as coherence, nor accept coherence as the criterion of truth, nor subscribe to the doctrine of degrees of truth, he *does* hold a form of the theory of internal relations. Some form of the theory of internal relations has usually been maintained by defenders of the coherence view (necessarily so, if our suggestion above is correct, that a coherence view of nature is necessary for a coherence view of truth), and it may be that the coherence theory of truth has been attributed to Spinoza because people supposed that the theory of internal relations, besides being a necessary condition for a coherence theory of truth, was also a sufficient condition. This *may* be the reason for Hampshire's claim, discussed earlier, that any metaphysical monism requires a form of the coherence theory. In any case, the theory of internal relations is often associated in contemporary discussion with the coherence theory of truth, and so Spinoza's accepting a form of internal relations has made it easy for people to attribute to him the coherence view as well. This attribution is made even easier by attributing to Spinoza a stronger form of the theory of internal relations than he actually held. It is suggestive that the period in which Spinoza became widely known was also a period of philosophical idealism, and that some of the most influential interpreters of Spinoza in English (Joachim, in particular) were men who were also defenders of the coherence theory. Leon Roth explicitly makes Spinoza the

---

[6] Haig Khatchadourian claims that a coherence theory of nature is a necessary condition for a coherence theory of truth (*The Coherence Theory of Truth*, pp. 27–29). On the claim that the coherence theory of nature does not entail that no proposition can be wholly true, see A. C. Ewing, *Idealism: A Critical Survey*, p. 221.

source of much that is characteristic of English idealism; in Bradley's *Logic* we have, according to Roth, "the mouth of Bradley; the voice of Hegel; the message of Spinoza." [7]

But we need not argue about whether the attribution to Spinoza of the coherence theory came about because some of his commentators wished to count him as a philosophical ally. I bring in Spinoza's idealistic interpreters here mainly to point out that the coherence theory in its modern form (that is, the conjunction of (1) coherence definition, (2) coherence criterion, (3) degrees of truth, and (4) internal relations) is fairly new, having been worked out by idealist philosophers since the time of Hegel. It is surely false to describe it as ". . . one of the two traditional theories of truth, the other being the correspondence theory," [8] unless we are willing to suppose that philosophical tradition is not much more than one hundred and fifty years old (and to overlook, in addition, much that has happened in the last hundred and fifty years). It *is* true, however, that some of the alternative theories of truth, common, or at least still familiar, while Spinoza was writing, were not nearly so common at the time Spinoza's work began to be taken seriously by philosophers. It may have seemed to some people in the nineteenth century that the only alternative to an empiricist correspondence theory was the coherence theory offered by the idealists. In any case, the ancient and medieval conception of truth as being had largely disappeared.

d. Truth and being

If we wish to see Spinoza's theory of truth in its historical setting, we must contrast the correspondence view not with coherence, but rather with theories of "truth of being" or "truth of things:" ontological truth. This view need not be a

[7] "Spinoza in Recent English Thought," p. 208.
[8] Alan R. White, article "Coherence Theory of Truth," p. 130.

rival of the correspondence theory; it can take the form of a more general theory which includes the correspondence view as a special case. Thus, truth, besides being a property of statements or ideas, can be a property of a variety of other kinds of things, such as actions or physical objects. Correspondence—saying that that which is is—is recognized as the form that truth takes in connection with statements or sentences; here we are dealing with "truth of statement." But on the most general level, truth is identified with being: things are "true" in so far as they *are*.

Theories of this kind can be found in ancient philosophy—in Plato and Aristotle—and in neo-Platonist philosophers like Plotinus. Making use of neo-Platonist views, Augustine worked out a theory of ontological truth that was extraordinarily influential. There is a statement of Augustine's theory in his Soliloquy, II, where he identifies truth with that which is; and he makes a number of other points, such as the claim that truth is its own criterion, that have analogues in Spinoza.[9] Theories of ontological truth are found in the Platonist tradition throughout the medieval period, in Anselm,[10] for example, and in Grosseteste, who refers frequently to Augustine and who sometimes offers formulations remarkably like what we find in Spinoza: "Truth, therefore, is that which is necessarily through itself or at least that which is the consequent necessarily to a being necessary through itself."[11] The ontological theory of truth does not end with the Middle Ages. It persists in early modern philosophy, and we find Descartes writing to Clerselier: ". . . veritas non distinguitur a re vera sive substantia. . . ." Further on in the same letter we find:

---

[9] *The Basic Writings of Saint Augustine,* ed. Whitney J. Oates, I, 277–97.

[10] "Dialogue on Truth," *Selections from Medieval Philosophers,* ed. Richard McKeon, vol. I, pp. 150–84. The two volumes of McKeon's *Selections* contain several writings on truth.

[11] "On Truth," in McKeon, *Selections,* I, 276.

"La vérité consiste en l'être, & la fausseté au *non-être* seulement. . . ." [12]

The similiarity of these views to Spinoza's should be obvious, since the thrust of our argument earlier in this chapter was to emphasize that for Spinoza the concepts of truth and of substance are closely connected. Self-subsistent being is both the ideal and the exemplar of truth. The truth of being or substance lies precisely in its *being* substance; that is, in its actual (formal) realization of the self-subsistent being that is posited (objectively) by the definition of truth or substance. Thus, the truth of being *qua* being is God or substance: when we are speaking of God, truth and being are the same thing.

Besides the identification of truth and being, truth is commonly identified with God in the Middle Ages. Anselm begins his dialogue on truth by saying that "Since we believe that God is truth, and since we say truth is in many other things, I would like to know whether we ought to affirm that wherever truth is spoken of, God is that truth." [13] Augustine also speaks of God as truth, and he offers an argument for the existence of God based on the fundamental and perfect truth which he says must necessarily support, and is implied by, individual true judgments.[14] Augustine's argument is, I believe, very similar in its logical structure to Spinoza's claim, in E-II, 45, that "Every idea of any body or actually existing individual

---

[12] Letter of April 23, 1649, eds. Adam and Tannery, pp. 355–56. Descartes, following scholastic usage, distinguishes intellectual truth (*veritas intellectus*) and truth of things (*veritas rei*). Thus, he writes to Mersenne: "Ainsi on peut bien expliquer *quid nominis* à ceux qui n'entendent pas la langue, et leur dire que ce mot *vérité*, en sa propre signification, dénote la conformité de la pensée avec l'objet, mais que, lorsqu'on l'attribue aux choses qui sont hors de la pensée, il signifie seulement que ces choses peuvent servir d'objets à des pensées véritables, soit aux nôtres, soit à celles de Dieu" (Letter of October 16, 1639, ed. Alquié, p. 144).

[13] McKeon, *Selections*, I, 151.

[14] "On the Free Will" (De Libero Arbitrio), Book II, in McKeon, *Selections*, I, 11–64.

thing necessarily involves the eternal and infinite essence of God" (Latin text, see p. 49).

Our introduction of Anselm and Augustine raises the issue of neo-Platonist elements in Spinoza's thought, which we shall have occasion to mention again in the next chapter. Note, however, that although neo-Platonist elements are fairly frequently pointed out in the fifth part of the *Ethics*, where indeed they are most striking, they are not confined to the fifth part; we find them also in the theory of truth. Some writers have claimed that neo-Platonist influence on Spinoza is most strongly evident in his early work.[15] Consequently it is not especially surprising to find that in the *Short Treatise* Spinoza connects God and truth more explicitly than he does in the *Ethics*. He speaks of "God, or, what we regard as one and the same, *Truth*" (*Short Treatise*, p. 78). Later he says that "*the Truth is God himself*" (p. 103).

I do not claim that Spinoza was familiar with the particular passages from medieval writers that I have quoted, but he was well-versed in medieval philosophy and it is likely that he encountered, if not these passages, then others expressing similar ideas. His library did contain works of Augustine.[16] I do not pretend to undertake a detailed exposition of the relation of Spinoza's theory of truth to medieval and ancient theories. The point I wish to make is simply that Spinoza's view of truth, as we have described it in previous sections, can be understood as a natural development of a very old tradition, with which Spinoza was incontestably acquainted, and it seems to me that his theory of truth is better seen as a version of ontological truth than as a version of the coherence

---

[15] See Carl Gebhardt, "Spinoza und der Platonismus," *Chronicon Spinozanum*, vol. I, pp. 178–234. Also Leon Brunschvicg, "Le Platonisme de Spinoza," *Chronicon Spinozanum*, vol. III, pp. 253–68.

[16] Number 17 in the catalogue of Spinoza's books is a folio volume described as "Epitome Augustini Operum omnium. 1539" (Freudenthal, *Die Lebensgeschichte Spinoza's*, p. 160).

theory of nineteenth- and twentieth-century idealism. If we *do* wish to compare Spinoza's position with recent theories, then the views of Heidegger,[17] or the "truth of being" of Hofstadter,[18] seem much more promising comparisons than the coherence theory. In the exposition of both of those modern theories, explicit attention is paid to medieval views.

An obvious question that arises in relating the ontological concept of truth to Spinoza is that ontological theorists could speak of a physical object as being true. But what does it mean for a physical object to be true according to Spinoza? Would Spinoza admit that truth can apply to anything besides ideas? To answer these questions we must examine certain features of Spinoza's ethical philosophy. When he speaks of objects, or of the ideata of true ideas, Spinoza does not speak of "truth" but of "freedom" and the question about the truth of physical objects is closely tied to the question as to whether, and in what sense, physical objects, including human beings, can be said to be free. The relation of truth and freedom, therefore, is the topic of the next chapter.

[17] See, for example, "On the Essence of Truth," in *Existence and Being*, pp. 292–324.
[18] *Truth and Art*, chapters 5–8.

V. Truth and freedom

IT REMAINS FOR US to discuss the relation of Spinoza's concept of truth to the specifically ethical portions of his philosophy. Spinoza says in Part V of the *Ethics* that "The highest effort of the mind and its highest virtue is to understand things by the third kind of knowledge" (E-V, 25), and "From this third kind of knowledge arises the highest possible peace of mind" (E-V, 27). These and similar statements are among the most famous in the *Ethics*. Clearly, Spinoza thinks that true ideas (which we have discussed in Chapter III) are essential to man's wellbeing; the theory of truth has *some* relation to ethics. But questions come to mind too. Why should knowledge, in and of itself, provide peace of mind? Why should knowledge be identified with the "highest effort of the mind and its highest virtue"?

The ultimate goal of human activity for Spinoza is freedom;

he opens Part V of the *Ethics* by saying "I pass at length to the other part of Ethics which concerns the method or way which leads to freedom" (E-V, preface), and in the next sentence he equates "freedom of mind" and "blessedness." A number of writers have pointed out that the guiding concept of Spinoza's ethics is "freedom," not "good." [1] Thus, instead of asking about the relation of knowledge to the highest effort and virtue of the mind, we may ask, "What is the connection between knowledge and freedom?" And since knowledge means possession of true ideas, the investigation of the importance of knowledge for Spinoza's ethical doctrine involves an investigation of the relation between truth and freedom.

According to Spinoza's theory that Thought and Extension are different aspects of a single reality, any "mental" event has a "physical" counterpart. Thus, improvement of the mind must be accompanied by improvement of the body, and logic and medicine could be called different aspects of a single science of human well-being.[2] Although Spinoza recognizes the relation implied by his doctrine between logic and ethics, or, in present-day terminology, between theory of knowledge and theory of action, his orientation is not that of present-day writers, even though they too have sometimes been interested in drawing parallels between knowledge and action.[3] Instead of presenting parallel theories of knowledge and action in which we can trace analogous concepts and problems in the two areas, Spinoza gives us a single theory of action and of

[1] For instance, Hampshire writes: "Because a thing's reality as a distinct individual depends on its activity and freedom, Spinoza must take the word 'free,' rather than the word 'good,' as the fundamental term of evaluation" ("Spinoza and the Idea of Freedom," p. 202).

[2] Spinoza is perfectly aware of this. In order to attain the chief good (summum bonum), he says that "We must seek the assistance of Moral Philosophy, and the Theory of Education; further, as health is no insignificant means for attaining our end, we must also include the whole science of Medicine" (*TdIE*, p. 6).

[3] See, for instance, Arthur C. Danto, *Analytical Philosophy of Knowledge*, pp. 53–54, 66–71.

knowledge, in which to know truly *is* to act, and vice versa. The analogous concepts are not all laid out side by side for comparison, but some of them are.

Spinoza tells us, for example, that the will and the intellect are one and the same (E-II, 49, cor.). Thus, the assertion of a true idea, which is an act of the intellect, and a free action brought about by the will turn out to be the same thing. We maintained above that "freedom," not "good," is a fundamental concept in Spinoza's ethics. Now, however, we see that truth too has a special position in Spinoza's ethical theory, since to have true ideas is to be free. Or. as Spinoza puts it,

§ Our mind acts at times and at times suffers; in so far as it has adequate ideas it necessarily acts; and in so far as it has inadequate ideas it necessarily suffers. (E-III, 1)

   Mens nostra quaedam agit, quaedam vero patitur, nempe quatenus adaequatas habet ideas, eatenus quaedam necessario agit, & quatenus ideas habet inadaequatas, eatenus necessario quaedam patitur.

Thus, to single out truth or freedom alone as the guiding ethical category is misleading. Freedom is fundamental in ethics, as truth is fundamental in logic, but at the deepest level the two are inseparable; there can be no freedom without true ideas, and no truth without free action.

Our discussion so far, although accurate, has perhaps been overly general. It is fair to ask for a more detailed account of the relation between knowledge and freedom; a more specific answer, that is, to the question asked at the beginning of this chapter, "*How* does knowledge lead to freedom?" Some writers on Spinoza have criticized him, saying that he does not provide a clear answer to this question. This seems to me unfair; whatever we may think of his position, he does give a fuller explanation than has usually been recognized.

To bring out the relation between truth and freedom in Spinoza, it will be convenient to divide our discussion into two sections, corresponding roughly to Part IV and Part V of the *Ethics*. In Part IV Spinoza emphasizes the limitations on human freedom. That is not to say that his discussion is wholly pessimistic; indeed, strictly speaking only the first eighteen propositions deal with "bondage." [4] Nevertheless, the free action discussed in Part IV is always subject to restriction or limitation by forces stronger than man.

In Part V Spinoza connects knowledge of the third kind explicitly with freedom or blessedness, from which it may seem to follow that to explain in detail the connection between true ideas and free action we ought to concentrate on Part V of the *Ethics*. But in fact the conclusions of Part V are prepared by, and in my opinion are fully intelligible only in the light of, certain doctrines that are set forth in Part III and Part IV. To see how it is that true ideas—the third kind of knowledge—lead to greater power or perfection of the mind, we must, I think, first indicate at least some features of Spinoza's theory of emotions, and of good and evil, as well as his concept of free action.

Besides roughly corresponding to the division between Part IV and Part V of the *Ethics*, the two sections of our discussion will also parallel Spinoza's distinction between the second and third kinds of knowledge, which he introduced in Part II. The second kind of knowledge arises "from our possessing common notions and adequate ideas of the properties of things"; the third kind "advances from an adequate idea of the formal essence of certain attributes of God to the adequate knowledge of the essence of things," and it is called "intuitive science." We should note that although both the second and third kinds of knowledge involve adequate ideas, only the third is based on "an adequate idea of the formal es-

---

[4] Spinoza makes this clear in E-IV, 18, note, which begins: "I have thus briefly explained the causes of human impotence and want of stability, and why men do not obey the dictates of reason. It remains for me now to show what it is which reason prescribes to us. . . ."

sence of certain attributes of God." Thus, although the second kind of knowledge can be reliable and certain, it does not give us an intuitive understanding of God's essence, and so it does not reveal the unity of truth and substance discussed in Chapter III. Nevertheless, the second kind of knowledge can be reliable, and it can increase our power of acting.[5] We shall proceed, after some preliminary discussion of "free action," "emotion," and "good" and "evil," to explain how this happens.

I

a. Free action

Something is "free" for Spinoza if it is unconditioned by anything outside itself:

§ That thing is called free with exists from the necessity of its own nature alone and is determined to action by itself alone.

---

[5] Spinoza's explanation of the three kinds of knowledge, as we have it in the *Ethics*, is as follows:

". . . we perceive many things and form universal ideas:

"1. From individual things, represented by the senses to us in a mutilated and confused manner and without order to the intellect (Corol. Prop. 29, pt. 2). These perceptions I have therefore been in the habit of calling knowledge from vague experience.

"2. From signs; as, for example, when we hear or read certain words, we recollect things and form certain ideas of them similar to them, through which ideas we imagine things (Note, Prop. 18, pt. 2). These two ways of looking at things I shall hereafter call knowledge of the first kind, opinion, or imagination.

"3. From our possessing common notions and adequate ideas of the properties of things (Corol. Prop. 38, Prop. 39, with Corol. and Prop. 40, pt. 2). This I shall call reason and knowledge of the second kind.

"Besides these two kinds of knowledge, there is a third, as I shall hereafter show, which we shall call intuitive science. This kind of knowing advances from an adequate idea of the formal essence of certain attributes of God to the adequate knowledge of the essence of things" (E-II, 40, note 2).

"Ex omnibus supra dictis clare apparet, nos multa percipere, & no-

That thing, on the other hand, is called necessary or rather compelled which by another is determined to existence and action in a fixed and prescribed manner. (E-I, def. 7)

Ea res libera dicitur, quae ex sola suae naturae necessitate existit, & a se sola ad agendum determinatur: Necessaria autem, vel potius coacta, quae ab alio determinatur ad existendum, & operandum certa, ac determinata ratione.

The distinction between "free" and "not free" does not hinge on whether there is a cause, but on what the cause is; if the cause is external to the agent, then the agent cannot be called free. Thus, a free action would be one in which the agent is the adequate cause of his own action:

§ I say that we act when anything is done, either within us or without us, of which we are the adequate cause. . . . (E-III, def. 2)

Nos tum agere dico, cum aliquid in nobis, aut extra nos fit, cujus adaequata sumas causa. . . .

(Spinoza does not talk of "free action," but simply of "action;" for him "free action" is a redundant expression. He defines

---

tiones universales formare I⁰. Ex singularibus, nobis per sensus mutilate, confuse, & sine ordine ad intellectum repraesentatis (vide Coroll. Prop. 29 hujus): & ideo tales perceptiones cognitionem ab experientia vaga vocare consuevi. II⁰. Ex signis, ex. gr. ex eo, quod auditis, aut lectis quibusdam verbis rerum recordemur, & earum quasdam ideas formemus similes iis, per quas res imaginamur (vide Schol. Prop. 18. hujus). Utrumque hunc res contemplandi modum cognitionem primi generis, opinionem, vel imaginationem in posterum vocabo. III⁰. Denique ex eo, quod notiones communes, rerumque proprietatum ideas adaequatas habemus (vide Coroll. Prop. 38 & 39 cum ejus Coroll. & Prop. 40 hujus); atque hunc rationem, & secundi generis cognitionem vocabo. Praeter haec duo cognitionis genera datur, ut in sequentibus ostendam, aliud tertium, quod scientiam intuitivam vocabimus. Atque hoc cognoscendi genus procedit ab adaequata idea essentiae formalis quorundam Dei attributorum ad adaequatam cognitionem essentiae rerum."

In *TdIE* Spinoza presents us with four, not three, modes of perception or knowledge (*modi percipiendi; TdIE* pp. 7–8, *Opera* II, 10). The four modes are not presented in quite the same order as in the *Ethics* (those numbered "I" and "II" in the *Ethics* are interchanged in *TdIE*), "action" in opposition to "being acted upon," or "passion," so that anything he calls "action" is free action. However, I shall use the term "free action" for rhetorical purposes, without intending thereby that for Spinoza there could be action, in the sense of the definition, that was not free.)

Note in addition that Spinoza can use the term "action" both for acts of the body and acts of the mind, and that the definition of "action" is the same in each case. Whether we, as human beings and finite modes of substance, can perform both—or either—kind of action is not yet at issue. What we wish to make explicit here is (1) that any event deserving to be called an *action*, in the strict sense of the definition, is *free*, according to Spinoza's use of "free" and of "adequate cause," and (2) that the term "action" can, in principle, refer to events conceived under the attribute of Thought or to events conceived under the attribute of Extension.

The question comes up at once, what are free physical actions, and can human beings perform them? According to the definitions, a free physical action would consist in an event or modification of substance, conceived through the attribute of

---

and the descriptions are not verbally identical. Nevertheless, the distinctions seem to be much the same. It is customary to say that in the *Ethics* the first two modes of perception of *TdIE* are grouped together as a single kind of knowledge.

This is all very well as far as it goes, but a question remains. In the *TdIE*, Spinoza numbers the four modes of perception straightforwardly from "I" to "IV." In the *Ethics* his numbering does not correspond to the kinds of knowledge; the passages numbered "I" and "II" are grouped together as the first kind of knowledge, and the third kind of knowledge is not numbered at all. We can explain this, I believe, by noticing that Spinoza introduces the modes of perception in the *Ethics* as ways in which "we perceive many things *and form universal ideas*" (italics added). His numbering corresponds to the ways in which we can form *universal* ideas: (I) From vague experience, (II) From signs, and (III) From common notions. These three ways of forming universal ideas can be separated into two types, those that give inadequate knowledge (I and II), and those that can yield valid results (III). Thus, Spinoza describes them as two kinds of knowledge, (1) knowledge based on opinion or imagination, and (2) knowledge based on common notions.

Extension, which was the cause of itself: "determined by itself alone." But only the physical universe taken as a whole is free in this sense. This is much like our claim in Chapter III that an adequate idea of a mode of Extension would involve a rational understanding of the whole physical universe. Indeed, if the will and the intellect are one and the same, these two positions may come to the same thing.

From all this it follows that we, as finite beings, cannot perform a physical action that is perfectly free any more than we can form an adequate idea of a finite mode of Extension, since the chain of causes is infinite. To perform a perfectly free physical action would require the adequate idea of the whole of extended substance, which we do not have. Only an infinite being could perform actions of this kind. But it does not follow that we can have *no* freedom, any more than it follows from our finitude that we can have no true ideas. However, the freedom we can have is a freedom of the intellect, not of the imagination, just as the true ideas we can have are

---

But intuitive science is *not* universal knowledge. It is knowledge of the (individual) essence of God (as we have argued in Chapter III). Therefore, Spinoza does not introduce it with a numeral "IV". Instead, he goes on to say that "Besides these two kinds of knowledge, there is a third . . ." The argument of our Chapter III provides some explanation of what can be meant by "an adequate idea of the formal essence of certain attributes of God." As confirmation of our suggestion regarding universal knowledge and knowledge of individuals, we have the statement of E-V, 36, note: "I thought it worth while for me to notice this here in order that I might show, by this example, what that knowledge of individual objects which I have called intuitive or of the third kind (Note 2, Prop. 40 pt. 2) is able to do, and how much more potent it is than the universal knowledge which I have called knowledge of the second kind" (. . . quod hic notare operae pretium duxi, ut hoc exemplo ostenderem, quantum rerum singularium cognitio, quam intuitivam, sive tertii generis appellavi (vide 2. Schol. Prop. 40. p. 2), polleat, potiorque sit cognitione universali, quam secundi generis esse dixi). We also have E-V, 24: "The more we understand individual objects, the more we understand God" (Quo magis res singulares intelligimus, eo magis Deum intelligimus), and the derivation from it of E-V, 25, seems to me to depend on an interpretation of the third kind of knowledge like the one I have suggested.

reflective knowledge (*ideae idearum*) and not ideas of modes of Extension. The two cases are exactly analogous, and the limitation on our freedom and on our understanding follows in each case from our finitude, which, of course, is a necessary part of our being as humans:

§ The being of substance does not pertain to the essence of man, or, in other words, substance does not constitute the form of man. (E-II, 10)

Ad essentiam hominis non pertinet esse substantiae, sive substantia formam hominis non constituit.

Thus, for Spinoza there are severe restrictions on human freedom; only certain kinds of free actions, namely acts of the mind, are open to us. The restrictions do not come about because of—or not only because of—Spinoza's definition of action as something of which the agent is the adequate cause. It is not at all uncommon to define freedom as the power of self-determination—the ability to act without external interference. Instead of being evident from the definition alone, Spinoza's restrictions on free action are revealed when we ask "what action (in the sense of the definition) is possible for a finite being in Spinoza's universe?" In other words, the restrictions on freedom are seen to follow when action is placed in its metaphysical context. We have here another instance of Spinoza's taking a definition which in itself seems compatible with other philosophies, and then developing it within a metaphysical system which leads to results very different from those of other philosophers. Although perfectly free physical action is impossible for humans, we can speak of some actions as *more nearly* free than others, and this brings us to Spinoza's theory of emotion.

b. Emotion

Spinoza offers the following definition of "emotion" (*affectus*):

§ By emotion I understand the modifications of the body by which the power of acting of the body is increased, diminished, helped or hindered, together with the ideas of these modifications. If, therefore, we can be the adequate cause of any of these modifications, I understand the emotion to be an action, otherwise it is a passive state. (E-III, def. 3)

Per Affectum intelligo Corporis affectiones, quibus ipsius Corporis agendi potentia augetur, vel minuitur, juvatur, vel coercetur, & simul harum affectionum ideas. Si itaque alicujus harum affectionum adaequata possimus esse causa, tum per Affectum actionem intelligo, alias passionem.

"Emotion" here is defined in terms of the increase or decrease of the body's power of action—that is to say, of its freedom, since, according to Spinoza's definitions, something is "free" to the extent that it is capable of action, and vice versa. The increase or decrease can come about through some external agency: in either case it is the increase or decrease in the body's power of action that determines whether there is emotion. The *source* of the increase or decrease—whether the cause is inside or outside—does not serve to define "emotion." We should not make the mistake of saying that the body is in a passive state whenever it undergoes emotion. This is the point of the second sentence of the definition. Emotions are not necessarily passive states of the body. *Some* emotions are passions, but the concept of emotion does not require this; there could be emotions that were not passions. Furthermore, we see from Postulate 1 that there can be passions that are not emotions, since some passions do not alter the body's power of action: "The human body can be affected in many ways by which its power of acting is increased or diminished, and also in other ways which make its power of acting neither greater nor less" (E-III, post. 1).

The point is worth emphasizing, because Spinoza is sometimes thought to maintain that all emotions are passive and that emotions are not found in a free man. That this interpretation is wrong can be seen from the definition we have quoted, which mentions the possibility of an emotion that is an action. In addition there is the explicit assertion of active emotions in E-III, 58:

§ Besides the joys and desires which are passions, there are other emotions of joy and desire which are related to us in so far as we act.

Praeter Laetitiam, & Cupiditatem, quae passiones sunt, alii Laetitiae, & Cupiditatis affectus dantur, qui ad nos, quatenus agimus, referuntur.

Where there is danger of confusing active and passive emotions, Spinoza is usually careful to distinguish, and he refers to passive emotions by such phrases as "emotions by which we are agitated" (E-IV, 15), or "emotions which are passions" (E-IV, 33). Furthermore, emotion is not something that applies to the body alone. Emotions were defined as "modifications of the body . . . *together with the ideas of these modifications*" (italics added). "Emotion" is well described by Hampshire: "The word *affectus,* although it comes the nearest to the word 'emotion' in the familiar sense, represents the whole modification of the person, mental and physical." [6] Thus, we can expect to encounter reference to emotions connected primarily with the mind, and to emotions connected primarily with the body.

c. Knowledge of good and evil

By "good" Spinoza means:

§ . . . that which we certainly know to be useful to us. (E-IV, def. 1)

Per bonum id intelligam, quod certo scimus nobis esse utile.

[6] *Spinoza,* p. 102.

And by "evil:"

§ . . . that which we certainly know hinders us from possessing anything that is good. (E-IV, def. 2)

Per malum autem id, quod certo scimus impedire, quominus boni alicujus simus compotes.

"Useful" here means useful in approaching the ideal we have set up of human nature (the free man), so a good thing is one that increases our power of action (our freedom). A bad thing lessens that power. Thus, good and evil are similar to emotions, since, like emotions, they are defined by the increase or decrease of our power of action. The passing of the mind to greater perfection (increasing its power of action) is defined as the emotion of joy; the passing of the mind to lesser perfection is sorrow (E-III, 11, note). But we have just seen that the same definition fits good and evil; they also are the passing of the mind to greater or lesser perfection. Good and evil, therefore, are the same as the emotions of joy and sorrow, and to know good and evil is simply to be aware of these emotions:

§ Knowledge of good and evil is nothing but an emotion of joy or sorrow, in so far as we are conscious of it. (E-IV, 8)

Cognitio boni, & mali nihil aliud est, quam Laetitiae, vel Tristitiae affectus, quatenus ejus sumus conscii.

"Knowledge of good and evil," which Spinoza introduces in the proposition we have just quoted, is of considerable importance in understanding the connection between Spinoza's theory of truth and his ethics. In the first place, knowledge of good and evil means possession of true ideas in the strict sense of Part II. For to know good and evil is to be conscious of an emotion (E-IV, 8, quoted above), and emotions include ideas. Indeed, Spinoza occasionally goes so far as to refer to emotions as "ideas:"

§ An emotion is an idea by which the mind affirms a greater or less power of existence for the body. . . . (E-IV, 14, dem.)

Affectus est idea, qua Mens majorem, vel minorem sui Corporis existendi vim, quam antea, affirmat. . . .

Thus, in knowing good and evil—in being conscious of emotion—the mind knows, or is conscious of, the *ideas* of the body's modifications; that is, we have *ideae idearum. Ideae idearum,* we may recall, provided the key to our interpretation of true ideas in Chapter III. That Spinoza intends the knowledge of good and evil to be understood as a case of *ideae idearum* is clear in the demonstration of E-IV, 8, which refers to portions of Part II where *ideae idearum* were discussed:

§ We call a thing good which contributes to the preservation of our being, and we call a thing evil if it is an obstacle to the preservation of our being (defs. 1 and 2, pt. 4), that is to say (Prop. 7, pt. 3), a thing is called by us good or evil as it increases or diminishes, helps or restrains, our power of action. In so far, therefore (defs. of joy and sorrow in note, Prop. 11, pt. 3), as we perceive that any object affects us with joy or sorrow do we call it good or evil, and therefore the knowledge of good or evil is nothing but an idea of joy or sorrow which necessarily follows from the emotion itself of joy or sorrow (Prop. 22, pt. 2). But this idea is united to the emotion in the same way as the mind is united to the body (Prop. 21, pt. 2), or, in other words (as we have shown in the Note, Prop. 21, pt. 2), this idea is not actually distinguished from the emotion itself, that is to say (by the general definition of the emotions), it is not actually distinguished from the idea of the modification of the body unless in conception alone. This knowledge, therefore, of good and evil is nothing but the emotion itself of joy and sorrow in so far as we are conscious of it. (E-IV, 8, dem.)

Id bonum, aut malum vocamus, quod nostro esse conservando prodest, vel obest (per Defin. 1 & 2 hujus), hoc est (per Prop. 7 p. 3), quod nostram agendi potentiam auget, vel minuit, juvat, vel coercet. Quatenus itaque (per Defin. Laeti-

tiae, & Tristitiae, quas vide in Schol. Prop. 11 p. 3) rem ali-
quam nos Laetitia, vel Tristitia afficere percipimus, eandem
bonam, aut malam vocamus; atque adeo boni, & mali cogni-
tio, nihil aliud est, quam Laetitiae, vel Tristitiae idea, quae
ex ipso Laetitiae, vel Tristitiae affectu necessario sequitur
(per Prop. 22 p. 2). At haec idea eodem modo unita est affec-
tui, ac Mens unita est Corpori (per Prop. 21 p. 2), hoc est (ut
in Schol. ejusdem Prop. ostensum), haec idea ab ipso affectu,
sive (per gen. Affect. Defin.) ab idea Corporis affectionis rev-
era non distinguitur, nisi solo conceptu; ergo haec cognitio
boni, & mali nihil est aliud, quam ipse affectus, quatenus
ejusdem sumus conscii.

Knowledge of emotions may appear to be inadequate
knowledge, for if there is an external cause of our bodily
modifications and we do not understand the external cause,
then to that extent we have a confused idea. But, although
we do not understand the cause of the change in our body
(E-II, 25), we do form ideas of the changes themselves (E-II,
22), which is to say that we can know whether our power of
action has been increased or diminished. And if we can con-
template these bodily modifications in themselves, that is,
without regard to their external causes, there is a chance of
forming clear and distinct ideas. Spinoza suggests this already in Part II:

§ I say expressly that the mind has no adequate knowledge
of itself, nor of its body, nor of external bodies, but has only a
confused knowledge as often as it perceives things in the
common order of Nature, that is to say, as often as it is determined to the contemplation of this or that *externally*—
namely, by a chance coincidence, and not as often as it is determined *internally*—for the reason that it contemplates
several things at once, and is determined to understand in
what they differ, agree, or oppose one another; for whenever
it is internally disposed in this or in any other way, it then

contemplates things clearly and distinctly, as I shall show presently. (E-II, 29, note)

Dico expresse, quod Mens nec sui ipsius, nec sui Corporis, nec corporum externorum adaequatam, sed confusam tantum, cognitionem habeat, quoties ex communi naturae ordine res percipit, hoc est, quoties externe, ex rerum nempe fortuito occursu, determinatur ad hoc, vel illud contemplandum, & non quoties interne, ex eo scilicet, quod res plures simul contemplatur, determinatur ad earundem convenientias, differentias, & oppugnantias intelligendum; quoties enim hoc, vel alio modo interne disponitur, tum res clare, & distincte contemplatur, ut infra ostendam.

The promise at the end of this note is not fulfilled until the beginning of Part V, where Spinoza makes it clear that sometimes we *can* separate emotions from the thought of external causes, and that we can thereby form true ideas:

§ So long as we are not agitated by emotions which are contrary to our nature do we possess the power of arranging and connecting the modifications of the body according to the order of the intellect. (E-V, 10)

Quamdiu affectibus, qui nostrae naturae sunt contrarii, non conflictamur, tamdiu potestatem habemus ordinandi, & concatenandi Corporis affectiones secundum ordinem ad intellectum.

The true ideas we have been discussing represent knowledge of the second kind. This is obvious in the note to E-II, 29, quoted above, where the mind is described as contemplating several things at once, and understanding "in what they differ, agree, or oppose one another." Such comparison of different things is a function of discursive reason, or the second kind of knowledge. Similarly, in E-V, 10, quoted above, Spinoza talks of "Arranging and connecting the modifications of the body according to the order of the intellect," again a case of discursive reason.

But knowing good and evil does not just provide information. It is a source of power for the mind itself:

§ . . . the mind passes to a greater or less perfection when it is able to assert of its body, or some part of it, something which involves greater or less reality than before. (E-III, general definition of emotions)

. . . *Mens ad majorem, minoremve perfectionem transit, quando ei aliquid de suo corpore, vel aliqua ejus parte affirmare contingit, quod plus, minusve realitatis involvit, quam antea.*

Also:

§ If anything increases, diminishes, helps, or limits our body's power of action, the idea of that thing increases, diminishes, helps, or limits our mind's power of thought. (E-III, 11)

Quicquid Corporis nostri agendi potentiam auget, vel minuit, juvat, vel coercet, ejusdem rei idea Mentis nostrae cogitandi potentiam auget, vel minuit, juvat, vel coercet.

Thus, knowledge of good and evil represents increased perfection of the mind, and this passing to a greater perfection may occur whether or not the mind has an adequate idea of the causes of the modification of the body. For, "The essence of the mind consists in knowledge" (E-V, 36, note), and so any increase in knowledge is an increase in the power—in the being or essence—of the mind.

A true idea contains the ground of its truth in itself; it is *free* in Spinoza's sense, since it does not depend on anything outside itself. If we understand something, that is sufficient to have free action of the mind. This is evident in E-III, 1 (quoted above), and in E-IV, 15, dem., where Spinoza speaks of desire which

§ . . . because it springs from our understanding something truly, follows in us in so far as we act.

. . . quia haec Cupiditas ex eo, quod aliquid vere intelligimus, oritur, sequitur ergo ipsa in nobis, quatenus agimus. . . .

Thus, to the extent that it can form true ideas of good and evil, the mind is free. But we have just seen that the mind can have adequate knowledge of good and evil even when it does not have adequate knowledge of the causes of the body's modifications. That is to say, the knowledge of good and evil provides scope for free action of the mind. There is a way even for finite beings to be free.

c. Linking of knowledge and emotion

The knowledge of good and evil is both knowledge *and* emotion. It is emotion because it represents an increase in the power of the mind, and it is knowledge because it involves possession of adequate ideas. As emotion it is related to other emotions, and it can restrain or strengthen them, and as adequate idea it is action, an assertion of freedom. We have here a uniting of action and emotion, making good the claim that active emotion is possible. The power of understanding, that is, of true ideas, in leading to a good life derives from their dual status as actions, free and self-determined, and as emotions capable of affecting other emotions.

The connection between knowledge and emotion is concisely presented in propositions 1, 8, and 14 of Part IV:

§ Nothing positive contained in a false idea is removed by the presence of the true in so far as it is true. (E-IV, 1)

Nihil, quod idea falsa positivum habet, tollitur praesentia veri, quatenus verum.

§ Knowledge of good and evil is nothing but an emotion of joy or sorrow in so far as we are conscious of it. (E-IV, 8. Latin text on p. 102)

§ No emotion can be restrained by the true knowledge of good and evil in so far as it is true, but only in so far as it is considered as an emotion. (E-IV, 14)

Vera boni, & mali cognitio, quatenus vera, nullum affectum coercere potest, sed tantum, quatenus ut affectus consideratur.

In Proposition 1, the note makes clear that Spinoza is using "idea" loosely to mean "image." He is making the fairly obvious point that the way a thing affects us, how it looks, for instance, is not necessarily determined by our knowledge of the thing. Railroad tracks *appear* to converge, although we know that they don't; the sun *looks* small, although we know that it is large. Proposition 8 connects knowledge of good and evil with the emotions, a point we have discussed above.

Propositions 1 and 8 are combined in Proposition 14, which is easily misunderstood at first. For if an emotion cannot be restrained by a true idea in so far as it is true, we might conclude that the power of ideas is not related to their truth or falsity, and that true ideas are no more useful in directing our conduct than false ideas. But that is not Spinoza's doctrine. Let us recall that truth is defined by Spinoza as correspondence (see Chapter III), so that when he says that no emotion can be restrained by the true knowledge of good and evil in so far as it is true, he means that we can know a state of affairs, or know the state of our body, but our knowing it does not change the facts. States of affairs are not altered by our knowing them. So far we have simply repeated the point established in Proposition 1. Now, we know that emotions affect other emotions:

§ An emotion cannot be restrained nor removed unless by an opposed and stronger emotion. (E-IV, 7)

Affectus nec coerceri, nec tolli potest, nisi per affectum contrarium, & fortiorem affectu coercendo.

But, by Proposition 8, knowledge of good and evil *is* an emotion (unlike most knowledge of states of affairs). So that in the case of knowing good and evil, knowledge *is* efficacious,

but its effect on other emotions comes about because it is an
emotion too. Spinoza makes this quite explicit in the first part
of the demonstration of E-IV, 15:

§ From the true knowledge of good and evil, in so far as this
(Prop. 8, pt. 4) is an emotion, necessarily arises desire (Def. 1
of the emotions, pt. 3), which is greater in proportion as the
emotion from which it springs is greater (Prop. 37, pt. 3). But
this desire (by hypothesis), because it springs from our understanding something truly, follows therefore in us in so far as
we act (Prop. 3, pt. 3), and therefore must be understood
through our essence alone (Def. 2, pt. 3), and consequently its
strength and increase must be limited by human power alone
(Prop. 7, pt. 3).

Ex vera boni, & mali cognitione, quatenus haec (per Prop.
8. hujus) affectus est, oritur necessario Cupiditas (per 1 affect.
Def.), quae eo est major, quo affectus, ex quo oritur, major est
(per Prop. 37. p. 3): Sed quia haec Cupiditas (per Hypoth-
esin) ex eo, quod aliquid vere intelligimus, oritur, sequitur
ergo ipsa in nobis, quatenus agimus (per Prop. 3. p. 3.); atque
adeo per solam nostram essentiam debet intelligi (per Defin.
2. p. 3.); & consequenter (per Prop. 7. p. 3.) ejus vis, & in-
crementum sola humana potentia definiri debet.

Another way of stating the proposition is to say that the
strength of true ideas does not come about because they correspond with reality, but because they increase our power of
action. True ideas do not change conditions in the world simply by corresponding with them; rather, they make *us* better
able to live happily in a world where those conditions obtain.
Knowledge of good and evil provides the link between
thought and action—between the intellect and the will.[7]

---

[7] That the best human life consists in living in accordance with nature, whose laws can be comprehended by study and improvement of
the power of understanding, is a doctrine with obvious Stoic overtones.
Spinoza's relation to Stoic writers would be a fascinating study. He pos-

These remarks do not contradict our earlier claim that for Spinoza perfectly free action is impossible. It may be, of course, that when we have true ideas our body is *more nearly free* than it is when we do not have true ideas, since it is then determined to action in a way that takes conditions into account. But this does not mean that our physical actions are any less related to physical bodies outside ourselves.[8]

This last observation—that our physical actions are related to and affected by other physical bodies—is important. For the increase in our power of acting that we have described is derived from emotions, and emotions are subject to influence by external causes. Since external causes are more powerful than we are, the degree of freedom that we can attain in this way is necessarily dependent on things outside ourselves. Thus, in propositions 15–17 Spinoza emphasizes the limitations on such freedom as we derive from true knowledge of good and evil:

§ Desire which arises from a true knowledge of good and evil can be extinguished or restrained by many other desires which take their origin from the emotions by which we are agitated. (E-IV, 15)

Cupiditas, quae ex vera boni, & mali cognitione oritur, multis aliis Cupiditatibus, quae ex affectibus, quibus conflictamur, oriuntur, restingui, vel coerceri potest.

---

sessed copies of works by Epictetus and Seneca. On Stoicism in the Renaissance, and on Justus Lipsius, who was a Renaissance interpreter of Stoicism (and whose edition of Tacitus was among Spinoza's books), see Jason Lewis Saunders, *Justus Lipsius: The Philosopy of Renaissance Stoicism,* esp. chapters III and IV.

[8] This interpretation of the power of the intellect is similar to that suggested by Morris R. Cohen: "His doctrine is rather the recognition that all rational effort involves an acceptance of the universe (i.e. we cannot improve nature except by nature's means). Hence there can be no true happiness or freedom that is not based on a recognition of the causal relation or necessary order which binds together the various parts of nature in time and space." ("Amor Dei Intellectualis," p. 11)

Nevertheless, true knowledge of good and evil does provide *some* basis for free action, or at least for action that is *more nearly* free than it would be without such knowledge, and as far as daily life is concerned this is as near to freedom as we can come. Spinoza devotes the rest of Part IV to the life of reason—that is, to the proper conduct of ordinary life within the limitations of our physical and social existence. We *can* speak of freedom in this context, but it is always subject to the restrictions of propositions 15–17. The freedom discussed in Part IV, therefore, is not the perfect freedom of the mind that we find in Part V. This is generally true, I think, despite places in Part IV where Spinoza seems to anticipate conclusions that are not made explicit until Part V.

We have talked so far of "knowledge of good and evil" as the key to understanding the relations between truth and freedom, taking freedom in the restricted sense of Part IV. But it ought also to be clear by now that any true knowledge whatever increases the power of the mind. This is to say that any genuine knowledge is knowledge of good, since any true idea represents an increase in the power of the mind, and an increase in the mind's power is what is meant by "good." There can be no knowledge that is *not* knowledge of good:

§ The mind . . . adjudges nothing as profitable to itself except that which conduces to understanding. (E-IV, 26)

. . . *nec Mens . . . aliud sibi utile esse judicat, nisi id, quod ad intelligendum conducit.*

If a thing worked to decrease the power of the mind, we could not form an adequate idea of it, for to form a true idea of it would *increase* the power of the mind, which contradicts the hypothesis that the thing decreases the power of the mind. Thus, there can be no knowledge of evil, or, as Spinoza puts it:

§ The knowledge of evil is inadequate knowledge. (E-IV, 64)
Cognitio mali cognitio est inadaequata.

We can be certain that something is good, for the same sorts of reasons that we can be certain that an idea is true, but we cannot be certain that something is evil. For certainty is *ipso facto* good: the possession of true ideas increases the mind's power of action, and whatever increases one's power of action is good.[9] Certainty, of course, is to be distinguished from the mere absence of doubt. (See E-II, 49, scholium.)

Thus, the expression "true knowledge of good *and* evil" is not strictly acceptable. Spinoza uses it primarily in the early propositions of Part IV that we have been discussing (for example, props. 8, 14–17). I think that the expression is intended to indicate the knowledge attainable by the mind of the body. Such knowledge is not the most perfect kind of knowledge, but it is necessary for the conduct of life, and it is the conduct of life that Spinoza is discussing in Part IV. The expression may also serve to make clear the distinction between active and passive emotions, and to establish true knowledge as the basis of free action. The contrast between active and passive emotions is clear, for example, in Proposition 15, and in its demonstration (quoted above).

The recognition that any true knowledge at all is a source of freedom leads us to the next section of our discussion. But perfect freedom could not be based on knowledge of the body, since the body is always subject to external forces. Consequently, in what follows we shall be concerned mainly

[9] This explains the different definitions of "good" and "evil" at the beginning of Part IV. "Good" there is defined as "that which we certainly know is useful to us," and it might seem that evil ought to be the opposite, namely "that which we certainly know is not useful to us." But Spinoza believes that we cannot have adequate knowledge of evil (IV, 64). So his definition takes a different wording: "By evil I understand that which we certainly know hinders us from possessing anything that is good." This is borne out by E-IV, 63, cor.: "We follow good directly and avoid evil indirectly." ("Cupiditate, quae ex ratione oritur, bonum directe sequimur, & malum indirecte fugimus.") Along with the relation between "truth" and "good" that I have suggested in the text, it is possible to work out parallels between "falsity" and "evil."

with the third, not the second kind of knowledge; that is, with ideas involving, as the basis of their truth, an intuitive understanding of the essence of God or substance.

II

a. Truth and freedom

Let us return to Spinoza's definition of "free": "That thing is called free which exists from the necessity of its nature alone and is determined to action by itself alone. That thing, on the other hand, is called necessary or rather compelled which by another is determined to existence and action in a fixed and prescribed manner" (E-I, def. 7. Latin text on p. 96). The phrase "determined by itself alone" suggests to us that what is free must be the cause of itself. And in particular, the phrase "exists from the necessity of its own nature alone" recalls the definition of *causa sui* as "that whose essence involves existence" (E-I, def. 1). It seems, then, that something that is free may be a form of *causa sui*. But we have shown in earlier chapters that there is a sense in which a true idea is a form of *causa sui*. If we now find that freedom also expresses *causa sui*, the relation of truth and freedom may turn out to be much more intimate than has hitherto been supposed. I believe that this is in fact the case—that truth and freedom are "identical" in much the same way that we have found truth and substance to be identical. More accurately, truth and freedom both express the essence of substance; they are different expressions—aspects—of the single reality or *causa sui*.[10]

[10] The terms "truth" and "freedom" are not satisfactory, theoretically. Spinoza uses them, but they are abstract terms, and, like all universals, aids to the imagination rather than names of things. For Spinoza, "truth" and "freedom" do not designate. When he is careful, as in his definitions, he speaks of "true ideas" (E-I, Ax. 6), or of "that which is called free" (E-I, def. 7). It is convenient to use abstract terms like "truth" and "freedom," but we must remember that this is just a way of discussing true ideas and free actions, and that there is no Truth and no

It is worth noting the similar language Spinoza uses in talking about truth, freedom, and substance. Compare, for example, the definition of "free," the definition of substance, and a statement from *TdIE* about truth:

§ That thing is called free which exists from the necessity of its own nature alone and is determined to action by itself alone. (E-I, def. 7. Latin text on p. 96)

§ By substance I understand that which is in itself and is conceived through itself; in other words, that the conception of which does not need the conception of another thing from which it must be formed. (E-I, def. 3. Latin text on p. 8)

§ . . . thought is said to be true, if it involves objectively the essence of any principle which has no cause, and is known through itself and in itself. (*TdIE*, p. 24. Latin text on p. 76)

Making explicit the connection between truth, freedom, and the essence of substance provides a way to understand the foundations of Spinoza's ethical doctrine.

We saw earlier that Spinoza defines truth as correspondence, but goes on to apply this traditional definition in a unique way. The correspondence relation, when it is fulfilled, is an identity; a true idea does not merely "reflect" or "correspond to" reality—it expresses the essence of reality—*causa sui*—itself. Similarly here, true knowledge on the one hand is theoretical knowledge which corresponds to states of affairs, and in so far as ideas simply correspond to something they do not change it (E-IV, 1, quoted above). But on the other hand, we can regard true knowledge as an increase in the mind's power of action. Since an adequate idea gives the essence of

---

Freedom apart from individual ideas and actions. The same observation applies to some other terms that Spinoza uses. It applies to "will" and "intellect," for example: "The will and the intellect are nothing but the individual volitions and ideas themselves" (E-II, 49, cor. dem); "Voluntas, & intellectus nihil praeter ipsas singulares volitiones, & ideas sunt."

causa sui, the action involved will be its own cause; "determined by itself alone," it will be free. Knowledge of good and evil, then, does not simply "provide the link between thought and action," as we said above (p. 109); rather, it permits us to see that adequate thought and free action of the mind are different aspects of one thing: "The will and the intellect are one and the same" (E-II, 49, corol.). One could say that truth can be seen from two points of view; in so far as it is a correspondence relation between two aspects of reality it is not a dynamic force, whereas in so far as it is considered as a manifestation of *causa sui* it is active and a source of power. But, of course, we could equally well say that freedom can be considered from two points of view: as a characteristic of actions that are determined by the nature of the agent, and as a source of truth.

It seems at first that if truth and freedom are alternative expressions of a single reality, then the difference between them may be like the difference between Thought and Extension, which are also different expressions of a single reality (E-II, 7, note). Thus, if true ideas express the essence of substance conceived through Thought, then perhaps free actions express the essence of substance conceived through Extension.

But in fact the difference between truth and freedom is not the simple one I have just suggested. We insisted above that "action" can refer either to action of the mind or action of the body. From this it follows that any interpretation that confines "freedom" to the attribute of Extension—to physical action—must be wrong. A glance at the latter parts of *Ethics* is enough to confirm this contention; Spinoza speaks constantly of "actions of the mind" and "freedom of mind."

This does not mean that the interpretation which makes freedom the counterpart of truth has to be abandoned. Truth and freedom *are* very closely related. What does, clearly, have to be given up is the suggestion that truth applies to Thought and freedom to Extension. We must say instead that truth and freedom are metaphysically identical, two aspects of the same thing, but that rather than being related as Thought and Extension they are related as idea and ideatum. For, as in the case of idea and ideatum, the distinction between what is true and what is free *may* coincide with the distinction between Thought and Extension, but it does not always do so.

But I do not think that the resemblance stops there. We have seen that something that is true and something that is free both express the essence of God or *causa sui.* We have further seen that a true idea agrees with its ideatum (E-I, Ax. 6). We know also that a true idea contains the *essentia objectiva* of its ideatum; in particular, we have the suggestive remark of *TdIE,* which I quote again here: ". . . thought is said to be true, if it involves objectively the essence of any principle which has no cause, and is known through itself and in itself." Furthermore, we know from E-II, 7, corollary, that

§ . . . God's power of thinking is equal to His actual power of acting, that is to say, whatever follows *formally* from the infinite nature of God, follows from the idea of God, in the same order and in the same connection *objectively* in God.

. . . *Dei cogitandi potentia aequalis est ipsius actuali agendi potentiae. Hoc est, quicquid ex infinita Dei natura sequitur formaliter, id omne ex Dei idea eodem ordine, eademque connexione sequitur in Deo objective.*

In this last passage, God's power of action is explicitly identified with that which follows formally from God. From all this it seems to me reasonable to say that truth is the *objective* expression of God's essence, freedom its *formal* expression. Thus, a true idea is the objective expression of a free action, or, a true idea and a free action are related as idea and ideatum. But both of them express a single essence—the property of being "in itself" or *causa sui.*

In our discussion of true ideas we said that to have a true

idea the mind must possess both idea and ideatum, and grasp their identity. In other words, the ideatum must be present in the mind: we have a case of *self*-knowledge.

§ The mind necessarily contemplates itself whenever it conceives a true or adequate idea. . . . (E-III, 58, dem.)

Mens autem se ipsam necessario contemplatur, quando veram, sive adaequatam ideam concipit. . . .

Thus, when we have a true idea, we could say that truth is the awareness of an action of the mind. The mind acts, in Spinoza's sense of "act," by asserting a truth (or self-evident mode of thought), and the possession of a true idea is the understanding of the act *as* an act; that is, as the cause of itself. Truth is reflective knowledge—the idea of an idea. There must *be* an act of the mind before it can be recognized as such, which is to say that we must have a true idea before we can know that we have a true idea: "in order to know that I know, I must first know" (TdIE, p. 12).

Like Thought and Extension, and like idea and ideatum, truth and freedom are identical from the point of view of substance; "metaphysically identical," in our earlier phrase. They designate two ways of expressing *causa sui*, which is the essence of substance. Their identity explains how understanding makes man free. Spinoza says in a number of places that the mind is not causally related to the body,[11] but this doctrine may seem to be violated by the claim that true ideas put us in the position to perform free actions. This difficulty disappears after the relation of truth and freedom is understood. Spinoza is not saying that first we acquire a true idea and then we can perform a free action, or that by having adequate ideas we can overcome our physical limitations. The free action involved *is* the grasping of the true idea. To un-

---

[11] For instance at E-III, 2: "The body cannot determine the mind to thought, neither can the mind determine the body to motion nor rest, nor to anything else if there be anything else."

derstand *is* to be free: every instance of genuine understanding—every act of the mind—is an assertion of freedom. This
is one way of interpreting the final proposition of the *Ethics:*

§ Blessedness is not the reward of virtue but is virtue itself.
(E-V, 42)
   Beatitudo non est virtutis praemium, sed ipsa virtus.

Thus, Spinoza can say that our freedom is in direct relation
to the true ideas that we have. "Our mind acts at times and
at times suffers: in so far as it has adequate ideas, it necessarily acts, and in so far as it has inadequate ideas, it necessarily suffers" (E-III, 1. Latin text on p. 93). The freedom
that is realized by true ideas is the only kind there is.[12]

b. Immortality

   Besides being the key to Spinoza's ethical theory, the view
of truth is the basis of his doctrine of immortality. The body
dies, of course, and with it the mind—that is to say, the idea
that has the body as its ideatum. Obviously, if there is no
body there cannot be an idea of an existing body. But not all
of the mind has the body as its ideatum. As we have seen, the
adequate ideas in the mind are ideas of ideas, not ideas of a
physical body. The reflexive knowledge that the mind has
does not die with the body. "The third kind of knowledge is
eternal . . ." (E-V, 33, dem.), and it will remain true, whatever the body does. For here neither idea nor ideatum posits
the existence of a body. If ideas of ideas—the third kind of

---

[12] Ruth Lydia Saw's conclusion that "Knowledge is the healthy activity of the mind, truth is the property of the ideas which the mind forms
when it is thinking well, and it is immediately recognized" (*The Vindication of Metaphysics*, p. 34) is, I think, suggestive and defensible,
given the background of an interpretation of Spinoza such as I have offered here. Unfortunately, in her arguments leading up to this conclusion, Miss Saw does not offer what I would regard as a sufficiently careful discussion of the conception of "truth" or of "activity," so that her
conclusion does not get the support it deserves.

knowledge—make up a significant proportion of the mind, then the mind will be largely immortal—which is to say that a large part of the mind will have attained the self-subsistent being of substance. This is an immortality of the intellect, not of the imagination, since imagination depends on there being a mode of Extension as the ideatum of idea. "The mind can imagine nothing nor can it recollect anything that is past, except while the body exists" (E-V, 21). Thus, it would not be a cogent objection, in Spinoza's view, to his conception of immortality to say that we can't imagine what it would be like. Spinoza admits that it is difficult to use the intellect alone, and no one can do it all the time. But that, again, does not count as an objection. We do *know*, in fact, some of this immortality, whether we can imagine it or not. Whenever we grasp an adequate idea we experience what Spinoza means by immortality. It is not, however, a self-conscious knowledge, and we cannot say "Now I am experiencing immortality." The moment we say this, we are regarding ourselves as separate modes, as individuals. Part of what occurs in Spinoza's view of immortality is that we forget ourselves as finite individuals; we are completely absorbed by self-sufficient (self-evident) truth—that is, by God or substance. Most people have had the experience of being completely absorbed by a thought or an idea, even to the point of losing awareness of their own individual status vis à vis the idea. To do this is to experience immortality:

§ . . . we feel and know by experience that we are eternal. (E-V, 23, note)
   At nihilominus sentimus, experimurque, nos aeternos esse.

Spinoza's program is to extend these experiences so that the part of us that remains dependent on imagination and the ordinary course of nature—our imagining ourselves as finite individuals—is "of no consequence" in comparison with the part that is immortal (E-V, 38, with its note). Spinoza does

not explain what he means by "of no consequence," but I do
not think that he has to be interpreted as saying that the
greatest part of our temporal existence is spent being absorbed in eternal truths. Temporal existence is irrelevant,
since by "immortality" and "eternal" Spinoza refers to things
that cannot be measured by ordinary temporal experience,
even if temporal experience be thought of as without end. As
he says,

§ . . . eternity cannot be defined by time or have any relationship to it. (E-V, 23, note)
   . . . *nec aeternitas tempore definiri, nec ullam ad tempus
relationem habere potest.*

It is more likely that Spinoza conceives a development in
which fewer and fewer of the ideas in the mind are unex-
plained. He strives for a state where he can understand
things instead of merely accepting them, and every new piece
of understanding is a step in this direction. Truth, paraphras-
ing McKeon,[13] (1) provides a means of freeing a person from
the passions and from his imagination; (2) is the highest
perfection (not only *man's* highest perfection but *the* highest
perfection, since truth is God or nature itself); (3) and it is
man's salvation. Grasping truth is uniting with God.

   There is another way of approaching Spinoza's view of immortality. Certain writers have made a distinction between
philosophies of being and philosophies of experience. Spinoza's philosophy is as pure a philosophy of being as there is;
truth itself, as we have seen, is an expression of the essence of
being. The temporal development or process suggested in the
concept of experience has no place in this philosophy; becoming has no status in the nature of things. Thus, the more we
grasp the truth, the more we understand of nature or God,
and the less significance we attach to time and to develop-

---

[13] *The Philosophy of Spinoza*, p. 307.

ment or experience, things which require time. We could say that when we understand the nature of substance we see that temporal predicates are inapplicable. Spinoza prefers to describe this aspect of substance by the word "eternity." Substance is pure being, not becoming. It *is*, and this is what is meant by its eternity. Or, in Spinoza's words:

§ By eternity I understand existence itself, so far as it is conceived necessarily to follow from the definition alone of the eternal thing. (E-I, def. 8)

Per aeternitatem intelligo ipsam existentiam, quatenus ex sola rei aeternae definitione necessario sequi concipitur.

The only thing whose existence follows necessarily from its definition is substance; eternity is the *being* of substance. But just as there can be true ideas that are less than the whole, there is a way of conceiving individual things as eternal. They are eternal in so far as they *are;* in so far, that is, as they share the self-caused and self-subsistent being of substance.

§ To conceive things therefore under the form of eternity is to conceive them in so far as they are conceived through the essence of God as actually existing things, or in so far as through the essence of God they involve existence. (E-V, 30, dem.)

Res igitur sub specie aeternitatis concipere, est res concipere, quatenus per Dei essentiam, ut entia realia, concipiuntur, sive quatenus per Dei essentiam involvunt existentiam. . . .

c. The intellectual love of God

It remains to be pointed out that there is yet another way of describing the phenomenon we have discussed—"the intellectual love of God." We have emphasized that when it contemplates an adequate idea, the mind is its own ideatum, and we have pointed out that entertaining adequate ideas is the same as free action of the mind. We have also claimed that both adequate ideas and free actions are manifestations of the essence of God. Therefore, when the mind has an adequate idea it understands its own power of action, and its power of action is thereby increased. This, according to Spinoza's definition, is an emotion of joy:

§ Joy is man's passage from a lesser to a greater perfection. (Def. 2 of the emotions)

Laetitia est hominis transitio a minore ad majorem perfectionem.

But adequate ideas also involve knowledge of God:

§ Our mind, in so far as it knows itself and the body under the form of eternity, necessarily has a knowledge of God, and knows that it is in God and is conceived through Him. (E-V, 30)

Mens nostra, quatenus se, & Corpus sub aeternitatis specie cognoscit, eatenus Dei cognitionem necessario habet, scitque se in Deo esse, & per Deum concipi.

We have, therefore,

§ joy attended with the idea of oneself, and consequently (Prop. 30, pt. 5) attended with the idea of God as its cause. (E-V, 32, dem.)

Laetitia oritur, eaque concomitante idea sui, & consequenter (per Prop. 30. hujus) concomitante etiam idea Dei, tanquam causa.

Since "love" is

§ joy with the accompanying idea of an external cause (def. 6 of the emotions)

Amor est Laetitia, concomitante idea causae externae.

we are justified in describing the possession of true ideas— freedom of the mind—as a form of love; the Intellectual Love of God.

Spinoza describes the intellectual love of God in one passage as

§ an action by which the mind contemplates itself. (E-V, 36, dem.)

. . . *actio est, qua Mens se ipsam contemplatur* . . .

And a little later he connects it explicitly with truth:

§ If there were anything, therefore, contrary to this love, it would be contrary to the truth, and consequently whatever might be able to negate this love would be able to make the true false, which (as is self-evident) is absurd. (E-V, 37, dem.)

Siquid ergo daretur, quod huic Amori esset contrarium, id contrarium esset vero, & consequenter id, quod hunc Amorem posset tollere, efficeret, ut id, quod verum est, falsum esset, quod (ut per se notum) est absurdum.

Since the love of God is the salvation of man, we can say that truth provides a means of salvation. But it would be excessively one-sided to do that, for we could just as well say that our salvation consists in freedom. (Spinoza at one point equates "salvation," "blessedness," and "freedom" (E-V, 36, note 1). Rather than claim an exclusive pre-eminence for the concept of truth, it is important to have shown the interrelation of the three fundamental concepts of Spinoza's *Ethics*— Being, Truth, and Freedom. The three concepts are fundamental in the sense that any one of them could provide a logical starting point in expounding, or in understanding, Spinoza's philosophy. Thus, it is not inconsistent with the unity of Spinoza's thought that he should at one time begin with the concept of truth (in *TdIE*) and at another with that of substance (in the *Ethics*).

The topic of the intellectual love of God raises again the issue of Platonist or neo-Platonist elements in Spinoza. There was an extensive literature on love in the Renaissance, much of it written by Platonist or neo-Platonist philosophers often inspired by the *Symposium*. A frequent theme was the power of love to raise man from preoccupation with bodily concerns to an experiencing of spiritual things, and ultimately, to unification with God. Associated with the discussion of love could be such other Platonist doctrines as the immortality (or eternity) of the soul, and freedom of mind as the result of a turning away from the body.

One of the most widely-read of the writers on love was Leone Ebreo, whose dialogues on love appeared in numerous editions in various vernacular languages, as well as in Latin. The expression "intellectual love of God" appears in Ebreo, and since a Spanish translation of *Dialoghi d'Amore* was one of Spinoza's books, it may be that we have here the source of Spinoza's term.[14] In any case, it is certain that Spinoza was familiar with Leone Ebreo, and his discussion of love in the *Short Treatise* has much in common with Ebreo's *Dialoghi d'Amore*.[15]

[14] Wolfson's unfortunate tendency to underplay Platonist elements in Spinoza can be illustrated by his treatment of Leone Ebreo. He writes that "Leo Hebraeus, in a classification of love which seems to be an elaboration of Aristotle's classification of friendship, describes that which Aristotle would call friendship of virtue as love based upon both moral and intellectual virtue . . . and as proceeding from right reason" (*Philosophy of Spinoza*, II, 304). Wolfson never tells us that the *Dialoghi d'Amore* were in Spinoza's library, or that "intellectual love of God" occurs in them. Instead he tries to make an Aristotelian out of Ebreo, too.

[15] For information on Leone Ebreo, see Carl Gebhardt's introduction to his edition of Ebreo's *Dialoghi d'Amore*, pp. 3–122. Gebhardt discusses Ebreo's relationship to Spinoza in "Spinoza und der Platonismus," and he gives reason for supposing that certain doctrines (although not the writings themselves) of Plotinus were known to Spinoza. "Und vom Geiste Plotins durchleuchtet ist das fünfte Buch der *Ethik*" (p. 217). For Renaissance views of love, with some attention to Leone Ebreo, see John C. Nelson, *Renaissance Theory of Love*, esp. Chapter II.

See also Léon Brunschvieg, "Le Platonisme de Spinoza." Brunschvieg contends that in Spinoza's early writing we find a sort of Plotinian neo-Platonism or "metaphysical mythology," and that the influence of Cartesian philosophy later brought Spinoza to a Platonism more akin to Plato's, in which mythical elements have largely disappeared and insight into reality is the result of a mathematical dialectic.

The presence of Platonist elements in Spinoza should not come as a surprise; and if it does it is perhaps partly because one of the most formidable works on Spinoza in English, Wolfson's *The Philosophy of Spinoza,* unfortunately tends to emphasize Aristotelian characteristics at the expense of others. I do not propose to discuss Spinoza's Platonism in detail (although that would be a fascinating undertaking), but the Platonist character of his theory of intellectual love as the salvation of man, of his theory of freedom of mind as the result of concentration on truth, and of the immortality of the soul should be reasonably obvious. In the *Ethics* the Platonist elements of Spinoza's philosophy are most in evidence in the fifth part, but, as we had occasion to point out in Chapter IV, they are not confined to the fifth part.

d. Concluding observations

Spinoza's doctrine that knowledge gives power is related specifically to his theory of truth; it is not simply another statement of the ancient view that knowledge provides a guide to right conduct. Many writers have said that knowledge is important for ethics; the more we understand of human nature, of the desires of others, or particular situations, and the like, the more, it is claimed, we will be able to act well. Thus, the more we know the better we are, either because knowledge enables us to act well (that is, knowledge is a means to some further end), or because knowledge itself is set up as a goal of conduct.

But Spinoza's position is different. For him, understanding is desirable not because it permits us to act in a praiseworthy fashion toward other men (although it does do that), nor is knowledge desirable only because it is a fulfillment of our proper activity or faculties (although here again, that is *part* of Spinoza's view; the essence of the mind *is* knowledge). Knowledge is desirable, rather, because it makes us more like God; more nearly independent and more nearly free. In knowing, the mind gives a particular manifestation of the free being of God, and approaches the status of *causa sui*.

We have seen that "good," the key term in many approaches to ethics, here becomes a secondary concept, having to do with the attitudes of men and not with the nature of things. It is nonsense to Spinoza to say that God is good; nothing is good in itself, and only finite beings could make a judgment of the form 'x is good.'

§ God is free from passions, nor is He affected with any emotion of joy or sorrow. (E-V, 17)

Deus expers est passionum, nec ullo Laetitiae, aut Tristitiae affectu afficitur.

We call things good if we like them, or believe them to be useful to us: ". . . we neither strive for, wish, seek, nor desire anything because we think it to be good, but on the contrary, we adjudge a thing to be good because we strive for, wish, seek, or desire it" (E-III, 9, note). Parallels could be found between Spinoza and present-day emotivists in the analysis of the word "good," since Spinoza believes that in calling a thing good we are really reporting its effect on us. But this does not mean that Spinoza has a wholly noncognitive analysis of "good," for the effect of a thing on us can be *known*, and this knowledge is a source of power.

Furthermore, there is no concept of moral obligation in Spinoza. People seek to persevere in their own being, and it turns out that this can best be done in a society where citizens behave humanely toward one another. But there is no *obligation* to behave humanely; each person acts according to what is best for himself. Spinoza recognized the revulsion that this doctrine would inspire in some of his contemporaries, and after stating it he interrupts his geometrical order to anticipate some of his later conclusions, as if to assure his readers that everything will be all right (E-IV, 18, note). Still, it remains true that, according to Spinoza, a person should live by pursuing what is useful to himself, and not by following some sort of moral law.

Instead of "good" and "obligation" Spinoza makes "truth" and "freedom" the fundamental categories of his ethical doctrine. But we have seen that truth and freedom are closely related—even identical from some points of view—and further, that both of them can be regarded as manifestations of substance or being itself. Thus, more basic even than truth and freedom, the concept of substance underlies Spinoza's ethics, as it does his metaphysics. One could express this in terms of present-day discussions and say that Spinoza bases his ethics on "is" rather than "ought."

But to say that Spinoza's ethics rests on "is" and not "ought" is not to say that for him whatever is is right, or that he fallaciously deduces "ought" from "is." It is to say, rather, that to *be,* in the sense according to which "being" means to be independent and complete, is the highest kind of existence, and the goal of human aspiration. To be true and to be free are simply different ways of *being* in this sense. To *be,* when we are talking of the "being" of substance, is an activity; existence is not something predicated of certain things, it is something things *do;* something that only God can do completely, that is, in every respect. Hence the frequent interchanging of phrases like "power of being" and "power of action"; the two are the same. One could say that for Spinoza the possession of true ideas makes us better not only morally but metaphysically as well. The more we know—the more we have true ideas—the more truly we can be said to *be.* This comes about because of the special conception Spinoza has of truth, and its relation to freedom and to being or Substance.

Spinoza's ethical views are consequences of his metaphysics and his logic—not of his conception of human nature. For human nature is not different from any other part of nature. Humans are complex, and they are conscious, and in this they differ from many other things, but the *conatus* or drive to preserve its being forms the essence, or power and virtue, of *any* individual thing, not just of humans. All things strive to preserve their own being, and to achieve the self-contained being of God or nature.

Bibliography

Works by Spinoza

Opera, ed. Carl Gebhardt. 4 vols. Heidelberg, 1925.

TRANSLATIONS
The Correspondence of Spinoza, ed. A. Wolf. London, 1966.
Ethics and On the Improvement of the Understanding, ed. James Gut-
mann. New York, 1949.
Spinoza's Short Treatise on God, Man, and His Well Being, ed.
A. Wolf. New York, 1963.

Bibliographies

Oko, Adolph. *The Spinoza Bibliography.* Boston, 1964.
Van der Linde, A. *Benedictus Spinoza: Bibliographie.* The Hague, 1871.
Wetlesen, Jon. A Spinoza Bibliography 1940–1970. Oslo, 1971.

List of works cited

Anselm, Saint. "Dialogue on Truth," in *Selections From Medieval Philosophers,* ed. Richard McKeon. Vol. I. New York, 1929, pp. 150–84.

Aristotle. *Metaphysics,* in *The Basic Works of Aristotle,* ed. Richard McKeon. New York, 1941.

Augustine, Saint. "On the Free Will," in *Selections From Medieval Philosophers,* ed. Richard McKeon. New York, 1929, pp. 11–64.

——. *The Basic Writings of Saint Augustine,* ed. Whitney J. Oates. 2 vols. New York, 1948.

Bennett, Jonathan. "A Note on Descartes and Spinoza," *Philosophical Review,* LXXIV (1965), pp. 379–80.

Bidney, David. "Joachim on Spinoza's Tractatus de Intellectus Emendatione," *Philosophical Review,* LI (1942), 47–65. (A review of Joachim's book.)

Blanshard, Brand. *The Nature of Thought.* 2 vols. London, 1939.

Brunschvieg, Léon. "Le Platonisme de Spinoza," *Chronicon Spinozanum.* Vol. III. The Hague, 1923, pp. 253–68.

——. *Spinoza et Ses Contemporains.* 4th ed. Paris, 1951.

Cohen, Morris R. "Amor Dei Intellectualis," *Chronicon Spinozanum.* Vol. III. The Hague, 1923, pp. 3–19.

Curley, E. M. *Spinoza's Metaphysics.* Cambridge, Mass., 1969.

Danto, Arthur C. *Analytical Philosophy of Knowledge.* Cambridge, England, 1968.

Deborin, A. M. "Spinoza's World View," *Spinoza in Soviet Philosophy,* ed. George L. Kline. London, 1952, pp. 90–119.

de Laguna, Grace A. Review of H. A. Wolfson, *The Philosophy of Spinoza, Philosophical Review,* XLIV (1935), 288–92.

Descartes, René. *Oeuvres de Descartes,* eds. Charles Adam and Paul Tannery, 11 vols. Paris, 1897–1913.

——. *Oeuvres Philosophiques,* ed. Ferdinand Alquié. 2 vols. Paris, 1963–1967.

Donagan, Alan. "A Note on Spinoza, *Ethics,* I, 10," *Philosophical Review,* LXXV (1966), 380–82.

Dray, William. *Laws and Explanation in History.* London, 1957.

Dunin-Borkowski, Stanislaus von. *Spinoza.* 4 vols. Münster, 1933–1936.

Ebreo, Leone. *Dialoghi D'Amore* and *Herbräische Gedichte,* ed. Carl Gebhardt. Heidelberg, 1929.

Eisler, Rudolf. *Wörterbuch der Philosophischen Begriffe.* 3 vols. 4th ed. Berlin, 1927–1930.

Ewing, A. C. *Idealism: A Critical Survey.* London, 1933.

Freudenthal, J. *Die Lebensgeschichte Spinoza's.* Leipzig, 1899.

Gebhardt, Carl. *Spinozas Abhandlung über die Verbesserung des Verstandes.* Heidelberg, 1905.

——. "Spinoza und der Platonismus," *Chronicon Spinozanum.* Vol. I. The Hague, 1921, pp. 178–234.

Goclenius, Rudolf. *Lexicon Philosophicum.* . . . Hildesheim, 1964. A photographic reprint of the Frankfurt edition of 1613.

Grosseteste, Robert. "On Truth," in *Selections From Medieval Philosophers*, ed. Richard McKeon. Vol. I. New York, 1929, pp. 263–81.

Hallett, H. F. *Benedict de Spinoza, the Elements of His Philosophy.* London, 1957.

Hampshire, Stuart. *Spinoza.* London, 1956.

——. "Spinoza and the Idea of Freedom," *Proceedings of the British Academy,* XLVI (1960), 195–215.

Heidegger, Martin. *Existence and Being.* Chicago, 1949.

Hofstadter, Albert. *Truth and Art.* New York, 1965.

Joachim, Harold H. *The Nature of Truth.* Oxford, 1906.

——. *Spinoza's Tractatus de Intellectus Emendatione.* Oxford, 1940.

——. *A Study of the Ethics of Spinoza.* New York, 1964.

Khatchadourian, Haig. *The Coherence Theory of Truth: A Critical Evaluation.* Beirut, 1961.

Kline, George L., ed. *Spinoza in Soviet Philosophy.* London, 1952.

Lalande, André. *Vocabulaire technique et critique de la philosophie.* 7th ed. Paris, 1956.

Lévêque, Raphaël. *Le Problème de la vérité dans la philosophie de Spinoza.* Strasbourg, 1923.

MacIntyre, Alasdair. "Spinoza," *Encyclopedia of Philosophy,* ed. Paul Edwards. Vol. VII. New York, 1967, pp. 530–41.

Martineau, James. *A Study of Spinoza.* London, 1882.

McKeon, Richard. *The Philosophy of Spinoza: The Unity of His Thought.* New York, 1928.

——, ed. *Selections From Medieval Philosophers.* 2 vols. New York, 1929–1930.

Nelson, John Charles. *Renaissance Theory of Love.* New York, 1958.

Parkinson, G. H. R. *Spinoza's Theory of Knowledge.* Oxford, 1954.

Plato. *The Dialogues of Plato,* trans. Benjamin Jowett. 2 vols. New York, 1937.

Randall, John Herman, Jr. *The Career of Philosophy: From the Middle Ages to the Enlightenment.* New York, 1962.

Roth, Leon. *Spinoza.* London, 1954.

——. "Spinoza in Recent English Thought," *Mind,* XXXVI (1927), 205–10.

Saunders, Jason Lewis. *Justus Lipsius: The Philosophy of Renaissance Stoicism.* New York, 1955.

Saw, Ruth Lydia. *The Vindication of Metaphysics: A Study in the Philosophy of Spinoza.* London, 1951.

Sextus Empiricus. *Outlines of Pyrrhonism,* trans. R. G. Bury. London, 1933.

Terrasse, Louis. "La Doctrine Spinoziste de la vérité . . . ," *Chronicon Spinozanum.* Vol. III. The Hague, 1923, pp. 204–31.

Urmson, J. O. "Ideas," *Encyclopedia of Philosophy*, ed. Paul Edwards. Vol. IV. New York, 1967, pp. 118–21.

White, Alan R. "Coherence Theory of Truth," *Enclyclopedia of Philosophy*, ed. Paul Edwards. Vol. II. New York, 1967, pp. 130–33.

Wolfson, Harry Austryn. *The Philosophy of Spinoza.* 2 vols. Cambridge, Mass., 1934.

——. "Spinoza's Mechanism, Attributes, and Panpsychism," *Philosophical Review*, XLVI (1937). 307–14.

Index